SELECTIONS FROM CAESAR'S
DE BELLO GALLICO

PREPARED BY ANDREW C. ARONSON
Sidwell Friends School

Longman

Selections from Caesar's De bello Gallico

Longman, 10 Bank Street, White Plains, N.Y. 10606

Series Editor: Professor Gilbert Lawall, University of Massachusetts, Amherst, MA
Consultants: Eric C. Baade, St. Stephen's School, Rome
              Robert I. Curtis, University of Georgia at Athens

Photo/text credits: Credits appear on page 92
Executive editor: Lyn McLean
Production editor: Janice L. Baillie
Cover design: Sally McElwain
Photo cover: Alinari/Art Resource, NY
Text art: Martin Walz
Photo research: Aerin Csigay
Production supervisor: Anne Armeny

Acknowledgments and dedication: Thank you, Sidwell Friends School, for giving
me the space of a sabbatical to finish most of this difficult text; thank you, Latin
students, for your opinions and critiques of the book; and thank you, Narda
Quigley, for spending part of your summer translating and proofreading the text.
I owe Martin Walz a large debt of thanks for his fine maps and timely help in
layout and printing. Professor Gil Lawall liberally and graciously applied his
editor's pen to the entire text; we are all the beneficiaries of his fine and intelligent
guidance. To Frances and Ralph Eyster, I thank you dearly for your generous gift
of time. To my parents and Edy, thank you now and always for your support
and encouragement. And to my wife Cindy and our sons Noah and Jesse, I lay
this book gently at your feet with all the love I possess.

ISBN: 0-8013-0976-x

20 21 22 23 24   V036   14 13 12 11 10

CONTENTS

INTRODUCTION

Who he was, or what he was, or what manner of man he was—no one knows for sure. Every age has carved its own Caesar, dressing him with its own passions and fears, tonguing him with the wit and wisdom of its passing moment. So we know of Caesar the tyrant and Caesar the merciful; of Caesar the killer and Caesar the lawmaker; of Caesar the wise and Caesar the lover; and of Caesar the Deified.

Theodore White

We come to know of Caesar in many different ways. We learn of him in famous plays, novels, and movies and through pithy sayings that have circulated for centuries: "Caesar's wife ought to be above suspicion"; "The die is cast" (**Ālea iacta est**); "To cross the Rubicon"; "I came, I saw, I conquered" (**Vēnī, vīdī, vīcī**); "Beware the Ides of March"; "You too, Brutus" (**Et tū, Brūte**); and "Friends, Romans, Countrymen, lend me your ears." We hear his name when we discuss autocrats: Caesar, Kaiser, Czar; and we hear it at the surgical delivery of a baby, a caesarean section. But we know him best by reading his *Commentaries on the Gallic War*, the subject of this reader, where in the exertions of marching and encamping, in the arena of fierce negotiations and diplomacy, and in the heat of battle, the gifted commander and masterful writer are brightly illuminated.

Gaius Julius Caesar was born into a patrician family of great lineage and diminished fortunes on July 13, 100 B.C. His family claimed descent from Iulus, son of Aeneas and grandson of Venus, but it was not the authority of his name or the aristocratic standing of his family that gave him political cachet. Of greater influence was the marriage of his aunt to Gaius Marius, Rome's most distinguished general and a seven-term consul. Often as Caesar climbed the **cursus honōrum**—in succession he was a legal prosecutor, military tribune, quaestor, aedile, pontifex maximus, praetor, and consul—he invoked the name of his uncle Marius and glorified him as a military savior and leader of the **Populārēs** in his speeches and writings. In truth, without the crucial reorganization of the Roman army that Marius masterminded—opening up the ranks to previously disqualified citizens, equipping the legions with more effective weapons and standardized marching gear, and reworking the deployment of the triple battle line—Caesar might not have succeeded in Gaul.

The year 60 B.C. was portentous for republican Rome. Caesar, Pompey, and Crassus, stymied by the Senate and each with different grievances and different ambitions, pooled their vast resources to form the First Triumvirate. In the following year Caesar took office as consul. He expertly guided new legislation through the Senate, or, when that failed, through the people's assembly, which had the power to enact laws. The Senate had already moved to thwart Caesar by announcing in advance of his consulship that it would award the consuls of 59 with minor posts overseeing Italian forests and grazing lands. Once more Caesar bypassed the Senate when a tribune in his service persuaded the people's assembly to award Caesar a five-year governorship over the provinces of Cisalpine Gaul (Italy north of the Po River) and Illyricum (located along the eastern shore of the Adriatic Sea). Additionally, to fill a vacancy in Transalpine Gaul (southern France), Pompey prevailed upon the Senate to assign Caesar that province too. In all, three provinces and four legions were turned over to him.

Caesar and his legionaries fought in Gaul for nine years. Caesar wrote his account of the war in seven books, one for each of the years from 58–52 B.C. After

Caesar's death, Aulus Hirtius, one of his generals, wrote the eighth book, covering the years 51–50. Each book was titled **commentārius**, the full Latin title of the work being *Commentarii de bello Gallico*. In form, though less complex and less detailed than the full-fledged histories produced by Caesar's contemporaries, the *Commentaries* are more than simple notebooks, which the meaning of the word **commentārius** might suggest. In them Caesar tells the events of the war, the historical causes, and the individual heroics with a minimum of adornment and maximum lucidity. Caesar the author disappears behind Caesar the commander, who in the Latin text is referred to in the third person. In regard to publication, we have no compelling evidence to prove either of two widely held theories, that Caesar wrote and published individual books annually or that he published the collected works in 51 or 50 B.C. on the eve of civil war with Pompey.

Note to the student: On the right hand page of the Latin are vocabulary review boxes listing at their first occurrence all words for each passage that either appear in the first two years of ECCE ROMANI, are formed from simple compounds, or are deducible from English derivatives. All review vocabulary should be learned since the majority of these words appear more than once in the reader. On the left hand page, an asterisk by a vocabulary word or idiom indicates that it will appear again; such words or idioms will not be glossed a second time but will be listed in the end vocabulary. Note that the perfect passive participle is given as the fourth principle part of transitive verbs, but for intransitive verbs the future active participle is listed. Finally, as a general rule, the vocabulary definitions proceed from general to specific; the final one or two meanings, therefore, will be the most suitable for your translation.

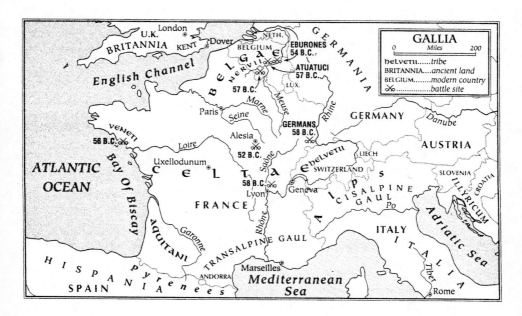

1   **Gallia est omnis dīvīsa in partēs trēs**: a famous opening, as commonly memorized and quoted as the beginning of Vergil's *Aeneid*, **Arma virumque canō, Troiae quī prīmus ab ōrīs.**

     Gallia . . . omnis: *Gaul, taken as a whole*, or *Gaul, viewed collectively*, or, possibly, *Gaul, in the larger sense*, since no translation captures the impact to a Roman of **omnis** placed after, not before, the noun it modifies, conveying at once that Caesar's subject is not merely the region **Gallia**, where the **Gallī** lived in central France, but the whole unconquered territory bounded in the west by the Pyrenees and the Atlantic Ocean and in the east by the Rhine River. Called **Gallia Comāta**, *Long-haired Gaul*, it included all or parts of modern France, Belgium, Luxembourg, Germany, Switzerland, and the Netherlands.

    ***dīvīsus, -a, -um**, *divided.*

    quārum . . . appellantur (3): supply words as needed: **quārum ūnam (partem) incolunt Belgae, aliam (partem incolunt) Aquītānī, tertiam (partem incolunt eī), quī ipsōrum linguā Celtae (appellantur), nostrā (linguā) Gallī appellantur**. A common feature of Latin is ellipsis, where a word is introduced and then understood in later instances (here, **partem, incolunt**, and **linguā**) or, frequently with verbs, saved to the end and understood in earlier instances (here, **appellantur**).

     A more natural translation of this relative clause into English might use the passive: *of which one part is inhabited by the Belgae. . . .*

    ***incolō, incolere, incoluī**, *to dwell, inhabit.*

2   ***Belgae, -ārum**, m. pl., *the Belgae* (a collective name for all the tribes living in the northeast region of Gaul, an area called **Belgium**, but substantially larger than modern Belgium).

    ***Aquītānī, -ōrum**, m. pl., *the Aquitani* (the inhabitants of **Aquitania**, located in southwest Gaul).

    ipsōrum linguā: *in their own language*, i.e., Celtic. Translate **nostrā (linguā)** similarly.

    Celtae, -ārum, m. pl., *the Celts* (referring to tribes occupying the middle band of Gaul, called **Celtica** or **Gallia**).

    ***Gallī, -ōrum**, m. pl., *the Gauls* (the Latin name for the Celts).

3   **linguā, īnstitūtīs, lēgibus**: *in respect to . . .* , ablative of respect. Latin often omits the conjunction between the last two nouns in a series; this omission of a conjunction is called asyndeton.

    īnstitūtum, -ī, n., *institution; custom.*

    lēx, lēgis, f., *law.*

4   **Gallōs . . . flūmen, ā Belgīs . . . dīvidit** (5): an example of ellipsis; the verb **dīvidit** needs to be supplied from the second half of the sentence and the noun **Gallōs** is understood in the second half.

    Garumna, -ae, f., *the Garonne* (a river in southwest Gaul).

    Matrona, -ae, f., *the Marne* (a river in central Gaul).

    Sēquana, -ae, f., *the Seine* (a river in central Gaul).

5   **dīvidit**: a singular verb is used for the two rivers because the Marne and the Seine are joined and together form the northern boundary of **Celtica**.

BOOK I

Caesar begins his account of the Gallic War with a brief introduction to the people and terrain of Gaul.

1. Gallia est omnis dīvīsa in partēs trēs, quārum ūnam incolunt 1
Belgae, aliam Aquītānī, tertiam, quī ipsōrum linguā Celtae, nostrā Gallī 2
appellantur. Hī omnēs linguā, īnstitūtīs, lēgibus inter sē differunt. 3
Gallōs ab Aquītānīs Garumna flūmen, ā Belgīs Matrona et Sēquana 4
dīvidit. 5

Comprehension Questions

1. According to Caesar, who inhabited the three major regions of Gaul? Refer to the map on page v to locate all regions and boundaries. (1–3)
2. What name did the inhabitants of the third region use for themselves? What did the Romans call them? (2–3)
3. By what three broad categories does Caesar claim that the people of one region can be distinguished from another? (3)
4. Name the rivers that account for the divisions of Gaul. (4–5)
5. How does Caesar offset the sense of unity in the words **omnis** (1) and **omnēs** (3) with a stronger impression of separation and division among the tribes of Gaul? What Latin words in particular create this impression? (1–5)
6. Caesar campaigned in Gaul with a rather small military force, roughly 50,000 men. As reflected in this opening description, what limitation within the Gallic nation did Caesar anticipate when he contemplated the subjugation of the whole of Gaul?

VOCABULARY REVIEW

ā or **ab**, prep. + abl., *from, by*
alius, alia, aliud, *other, another*
appellō, -āre, -āvī, -ātus, *to name, call*
differō, differre, distulī, dīlātus, irreg., *to differ, vary*
dīvidō, -ere, dīvīsī, dīvīsus, *to divide, separate*
et, conj., *and*
flūmen, flūminis, n., *river*
Gallia, -ae, f., *Gaul*
hic, haec, hoc, *this*
in, prep. + acc., *into*
inter, prep. + acc., *between, among*

ipse, ipsa, ipsum, *himself, herself, itself, themselves*
lingua, -ae, f., *tongue; language*
noster, nostra, nostrum, *our*
omnis, -is, -e, *all; the entire; each*
pars, partis, f., *part*
quī, quae, quod, *who, which, that*
sē, *himself, herself, itself, themselves*
sum, esse, fuī, futūrus, irreg., *to be*
tertius, -a, -um, *third*
trēs, trēs, tria, trium, *three*
ūnus, -a, -um, *one*

6   **Hōrum omnium**: i.e., the Gallic people, picking up **hī omnēs** in line 3. **Hōrum** is what case, number, and gender of **hic**?

    ***proptereā quod**, idiom, *because;* lit., *because of the fact that.*

    cultus, -ūs, m., *cultivation; standard of living; civilization.*

7   **hūmānitās, hūmānitātis**, f., *humane character, moral refinement.*

    prōvincia, -ae, f., *province.*

        Here, specifically, the Province (modern Provence), a strategic strip of land extending from the Pyrenees and the Garonne to the Rhône River, taken militarily from the Gauls by the Romans in 121–120 B.C. and awarded to Caesar as part of his proconsulship in 58 B.C. The province was also known as **Gallia Narbōnensis** from its capital at Narbo.

    minimē: translate with **saepe** (8), *least often = very seldom.*

8   **mercātōrēs**: nominative plural; a reference to traders from the Province.

    commeō, -āre, -āvī, -ātūrus, *to go back and forth;* + **ad** + acc., *to reach.*

    ea: *those goods*, object of **important** (9).

    effēminō, -āre, -āvī, -ātus, *to remove one's manliness; to weaken.*

        ad effēminandōs animōs: *to dull the fighting spirit*, gerundive of purpose with **ad**.

9   **pertineō, -ēre, -uī**, *to extend; to tend.*

    importō, -āre, -āvī, -ātus, *to bring in; to introduce* (for sale).

    ***proximus, -a, -um** + dat., *nearest (to), closest (to).*

        proximīque sunt . . . gerunt (10): Caesar gives this as his third reason for the superiority of the Belgae over the other Gauls: *and (because) they are. . . .*

    ***Rhēnus, -ī**, m., *the Rhine* (the major north-south river that marked the boundary between Gaul and Germany).

10   **continenter**, adv., *continually.*

    Quā dē causā: *For this reason;* lit., *Concerning which reason.*

    ***Helvētius, -a, -um**, *of the Helvetii, Helvetian;* m. pl., *the Helvetii* (a tribe from the central region of Gaul against which Caesar will have his first military encounter).

11   ***virtūs, virtūtis**, f., *courage, bravery.*

    virtūte: for the ablative of respect, see page 2, note to line 3.

    praecēdō, praecēdere, praecessī, praecessūrus, *to go before; to surpass.*

    cotīdiānus, -a, -um, *daily.*

    ***proelium, -ī**, n., *battle, skirmish.*

    cotīdiānīs proeliīs: *by means of . . .* or *in . . .*, ablative of means.

12   ***contendō, contendere, contendī, contentus**, *to struggle, fight, clash.*

    ***fīnis, fīnis, fīnium**, m., *end; boundary;* pl., *borders, territory.*

    eōs . . . eōrum (13): referring to the Germans in both cases.

    ***prohibeō, -ēre, -uī, -itus**, *to prevent; to keep* X (acc. of direct object) *away from* Y (abl. of separation).

        cum aut . . . prohibent aut ipsī . . . gerunt (13): *whenever they* (i.e., the Helvetii) *either are keeping . . . or are themselves waging. . . .* The mood of the verb in a **cum** clause is indicative if the clause refers to events in the present or future, and if it denotes a repeated action.

Caesar singles out two Gallic tribes for their superiority in battle.

Hōrum omnium fortissimī sunt Belgae, proptereā quod ā cultū 6
atque hūmānitāte prōvinciae longissimē absunt, minimēque ad eōs 7
mercātōrēs saepe commeant atque ea, quae ad effēminandōs animōs 8
pertinent, important; proximīque sunt Germānīs, quī trāns Rhēnum 9
incolunt, quibuscum continenter bellum gerunt. Quā dē causā Helvētiī 10
quoque reliquōs Gallōs virtūte praecēdunt, quod ferē cotīdiānīs proeliīs 11
cum Germānīs contendunt, cum aut suīs fīnibus eōs prohibent aut ipsī 12
in eōrum fīnibus bellum gerunt. 13

Caesar, *De bello Gallico* I.1

Comprehension Questions

1. Why in Caesar's opinion were the Belgae the bravest of the Gauls? (6–10)
2. What is the essential difference between **cultus** (6) and **hūmānitās** (7)? How would the presence or absence of either one affect the culture and behavior of a people?
3. What material goods do you think might have contributed to a general weakening of a tribe's moral and military strength? (8–9)
4. The Belgae and the Helvetii proved to be very tough opponents for Caesar. How did the geography of Gaul influence their military prowess? By implication, who might be a tougher opponent than either tribe? (9–13)

VOCABULARY REVIEW

absum, abesse, āfuī, āfutūrus, irreg., *to be away*
ad, prep. + acc., *to, toward; at*
animus, -ī, m., *mind; spirit, courage*
atque, conj., *and*
aut . . . aut, conj., *either . . . or*
bellum, -ī, n., *war*
causa, -ae, f., *cause, reason*
cum, prep. + abl., *with*
cum, conj., *when; since*
dē, prep. + abl., *down from; about, concerning*
ferē, adv., *nearly, almost*
fortis, -is, -e, *strong; brave*
Germānī, -ōrum, m. pl., *the Germans*
gerō, -ere, gessī, gestus, *to carry; to conduct; to wage*

in, prep. + abl., *in, on*
is, ea, id, *he, she, it; this, that*
longē, adv., *far*
mercātor, mercātōris, m., *merchant, trader*
minimē, adv., *very little, the least*
-que, conj., *and*
quī, quae, quod, interrog. adj., *what, which*
quod, conj., *because*
quoque, adv., *also, too*
reliquus, -a, -um, *remaining, the rest of*
saepe, adv., *often*
suus, -a, -um, *his, her, its, their (own)*
trāns, prep. + acc., *across*

BOOK I: TROUBLE IN THE PROVINCE

Four hundred years of conflict, uneasy alliances, and mutual enrichment between Rome and the tribes of Gaul preceded Caesar's Gallic campaign. These foreigners, called *Keltoi* by the Greeks and **Gallī** by the Romans, began to pour across the Alps from their homes in Switzerland and Germany in the fifth century B.C. They were attracted to the rich farm land in the Po valley and they fought as mercenaries within Italy.

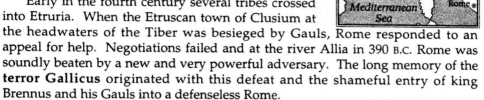

Early in the fourth century several tribes crossed into Etruria. When the Etruscan town of Clusium at the headwaters of the Tiber was besieged by Gauls, Rome responded to an appeal for help. Negotiations failed and at the river Allia in 390 B.C. Rome was soundly beaten by a new and very powerful adversary. The long memory of the **terror Gallicus** originated with this defeat and the shameful entry of king Brennus and his Gauls into a defenseless Rome.

Gallic tribes began to hire themselves out to Roman enemies, and Rome in turn began appropriating good farm land and establishing trade centers in the north of Italy. Both developments led to bloody conflicts and to an emerging consensus in Rome that the Gallic threat in Italy would have to be defused. The battle of Telamon in 232 B.C., a Roman victory and stinging defeat for the combined Gallic forces, was a turning point in Gallo-Roman relations. Rome took the offensive and by the 180's she had either subjugated the Gallic tribes in the Po region or turned them into loyal allies.

Meanwhile, Roman interest in southern Gaul had grown in the third century, spurred on by a strong Carthaginian presence in Spain during the second Punic War. The Rhône valley had already been an area of much activity in the preceding centuries, benefiting from the introduction of Greek culture and trade through the popular seaport of Marseilles.

In 125 B.C. Marseilles called upon the Romans to help them in dealing with the Saluvii, a tribe which dominated the Alpine passes and was pressing westward. The Romans vigorously turned back the Saluvii and destroyed their capital city. A new Roman settlement, Aquae Sextiae, became a base of operations for further Roman expansion. By 121 the Romans had defeated two other belligerent tribes, the Allobroges and Arverni, incorporating the former into the new Roman province of Transalpine Gaul and drawing the latter into the Roman sphere of influence. The Romans also entered into formal alliances with the Aedui and the Sequani along the northern reaches of the Rhône River.

The first large threat to the stability of the Province in southern Gaul came at the end of the second century as a wave of northerners called the Cimbri and Teutones swept down from their homes north of the Danube, uprooting tribes in their way and harassing Roman allies in the Province. Roman opposition to them failed miserably until the command was turned over to Marius, who defeated the Teutones at Aquae Sextiae in 102 and the Cimbri in the following year. The memory of earlier Gallic invasions in the heartland of Italy coupled with this recent experience of Germanic invaders on the northern borders of Italy would soon give Caesar apparent just cause in using force to meet foreign threats to Rome and her allies in the Alpine provinces. Caesar was personally connected to the war with the Germans by the presence on the battlefield of his uncle Marius, and through his third wife Calpurnia, whose great-grandfather L. Calpurnius Piso was killed in an ambush in 107 at the hands of the Tigurini, an Helvetian tribal clan who had accompanied the Cimbri and Teutones in their drive south.

The germ of the Gallic War was contained in a decision in 60 B.C. by the Helvetii to migrate en masse from their home in Switzerland to a more promising home in western Gaul. The plan was devised by a nobleman, Orgetorix, who, according to Caesar, played on a popular sentiment that the small compass of Helvetia, penned in by natural boundaries, was insufficient to meet the collective needs and military ambitions of the people. But in a secret pact with Casticus of the Sequani tribe and Dumnorix of the Aedui, Orgetorix sought greater power by promising to install his co-conspirators as tribal kings and establish a ruling triumvirate over all of Gaul. The plot was exposed and although Orgetorix used his considerable influence to avoid trial, he died soon after.

> After the death of Orgetorix, the Helvetii did not abandon their attempts to move out of their territory as they had determined to do. When they eventually thought they were ready to start the migration, they set fire to all their **oppida**, about 12 altogether, and to some 400 villages and the individual buildings that remained. They burned all the grain, except for what they intended to take with them.
>
> Caesar, *De bello Gallico*, I.5

Of the two routes available to them out of Helvetia—one upstream over a narrow river pass in the land of the Sequani, the second south over easier terrain but in the Roman Province—they chose the southern route and planned to force their way through the land of the Allobroges. Caesar, now governor, learned of this while still in Rome and with characteristic speed reached Geneva before the Helvetii were set to depart on March 28th, 58 B.C. Caesar told the Helvetii that he needed two weeks to decide on their request to pass through the Province and then he used that time to build walls, trenches and manned posts along the Rhone to prevent such a passage. The Helvetii countered by engaging the Aeduan Dumnorix to win permission from the Sequani to pass through their land.

Caesar left his chief lieutenant Labienus in charge of the 10th legion at Geneva and returned to Cisalpine Gaul, where he summoned three standing legions and recruited two more. With five legions he crossed the Alps and set up camp at the confluence of the Saône and Rhône rivers near Lyon.

> The Helvetii had already led their forces through the pass in the country of the Sequani and had reached that of the Aedui and were pillaging it. Since the Aedui could not defend themselves or their property from them, they sent envoys to Caesar to ask for help.
>
> They pointed out that they had always been loyal to Rome and so it was not right that their land was being laid waste, their children led off into slavery, and their **oppida** taken by storm under the very eyes of his army....
>
> Prompted by these complaints, Caesar decided that he must not delay; if he did, everything that our allies owned would be destroyed, and the Helvetii would get through to the country of the Santones.
>
> Caesar, *De bello Gallico*, I.11

1 *__Arar, Araris__, acc., __Ararim__, m., *the Saône* (a tributary of the Rhône).
   *__Aeduī, -ōrum__, m. pl., *the Aedui* (a tribe living near the Saone River).
   *__Sēquanī, -ōrum__, m. pl., *the Sequani* (a tribe north of the Aedui).
2 __Rhodanus, -ī__, m., *the Rhône* (a major north-south river).
   __īnfluō, īnfluere, īnflūxī, īnfluxūrus__, *to flow in, flow.*
   __lēnitās, lēnitātis__, f., *gentleness;* of water, *sluggishness, slowness.*
      __incrēdibilī lēnitāte:__ *(a river) of* . . . , ablative of description.
   __ita ut . . . possit__ (3): the actual subject of __possit__ is the clause __in utram partem fluat,__ but translate __nōn possit__ impersonally as *it cannot.*
   *__uter, utra, utrum__, *which* (of two).
   __partem:__ *direction.*
   __fluō, fluere, flūxī, flūxūrus__, *to flow.*
3 *__iūdicō, -āre, -āvī, -ātus__, *to judge, decide, determine.*
   __Id:__ i.e., the river. What case and number is the pronoun?
   __ratis, ratis, ratium__, f., *raft.*
   *__linter, lintris__, f., *canoe.*
4 __explōrātor, explōrātōris__, m., *scout;* pl., *scouting party, patrol.*
   __Caesar certior factus est:__ *Caesar was made more certain (that)* = *Caesar was informed (that)* . . . , *Caesar learned (that).* . . .
   __trēs . . . trādūxisse__ (5): within an indirect statement the direct object of the infinitive will often precede the subject of the infinitive, as here. Note that the prefix __trā-__ for __trāns__ in __trādūxisse__ governs __id flūmen__ and makes a preposition there unnecessary.
   __trēs . . . partēs:__ *three quarters.*
   *__cōpiae, -ārum__, f. pl., *troops.*
5 __quārtam vērō partem:__ *(but that) in fact the fourth part.* . . . ; an example of asyndeton. For the device, see page 2, note to line 3.
   __citrā__, prep. + acc., *on this side of, on the near* (= Roman) *side of.*
6 *__dē:__ in temporal phrases: *at the start of; just after.*
   *__vigilia, -ae__, f., *watch.*
      The period from sunset to sunrise was divided into four watches, called __vigiliae__, of three hours each; the third watch would have run from approximately midnight to 3 A.M.
   *__castra, -ōrum__, n. pl., *camp.*
8 __impedītus, -a, -um__, *hindered, hampered; encumbered with supplies.*
   __inopīnāns, inopīnantis__, *unaware, caught off guard.*
   __aggredior, aggredī, aggressus sum__, *to approach; to go against, attack.*
   __concīdō, concīdere, concīdī, concīsus__, *to cut up; to kill.*
9 *__sēsē:__ an alternate form of the reflexive pronoun __sē__, *themselves.*
   __mandō, -āre, -āvī, -ātus__, *to hand over.*
      __sēsē fugae mandārunt__ (= __mandāvērunt__): *they handed themselves over to flight* = *they took flight, they fled.*
   *__abdō, abdere, abdidī, abditus__, *to put away, conceal;* + __sē__, *to hide oneself.*
      __in proximās silvās abdidērunt:__ repeat __sēsē__ with __abdidērunt__. Caesar uses __in__ + acc. because the verb __abdere__ contains the idea of motion towards; you may catch this by adding a verb of motion in your translation: *(entering) into* . . . *they.* . . .

Caesar leads a surprise raid on the rear forces of the Helvetii at the river Saône.

12. Flūmen est Arar, quod per fīnēs Aeduōrum et Sēquanōrum in 1
Rhodanum īnfluit, incrēdibilī lēnitāte ita ut oculīs in utram partem fluat 2
iūdicārī nōn possit. Id Helvētiī ratibus ac lintribus iūnctīs trānsībant. 3
Ubi per explōrātōrēs Caesar certior factus est trēs iam partēs cōpiārum 4
Helvētiōs id flūmen trādūxisse, quārtam vērō partem citrā flūmen 5
Ararim reliquam esse, dē tertiā vigiliā cum legiōnibus tribus ē castrīs 6
profectus ad eam partem pervēnit, quae nōndum flūmen trānsierat. Eōs 7
impedītōs et inopīnantēs aggressus magnam partem eōrum concīdit; 8
reliquī sēsē fugae mandārunt atque in proximās silvās abdidērunt. 9

Comprehension Questions

1. Why did the Helvetii choose this place in the river to transport their entire population? How were they crossing the river? (1–3)
2. What did Caesar learn from his patrol? (4–6)
3. When and with how many troops did Caesar leave the camp? (6–7)
4. Why did Caesar succeed so well in his surprise attack? How does the word order emphasize the effectiveness of his attack? (7–9)

VOCABULARY REVIEW

ac, conj., *and*
Caesar, Caesaris, m., *Caesar*
certus, -a, -um, *certain*
ē or **ex**, prep. + abl., *from, out of*
faciō, -ere, fēcī, factus, *to make; to do*
fuga, -ae, f., *flight*
iam, adv., *now, already*
incrēdibilis, -is, -e, *incredible, remarkable*
ita, adv., *thus; so, in such a way*
iungō, -ere, iūnxī, iūnctus, *to join, fasten together*
legiō, legiōnis, f., *legion*
magnus, -a, -um, *big, large, great*
nōn, adv., *not*
nōndum, adv., *not yet*
oculus, -ī, m., *eye*
per, prep. + acc., *through*

perveniō, -īre, pervēnī, perventūrus + **ad** + acc., *to arrive at, reach*
possum, posse, potuī, irreg., *to be able, can*
proficīscor, proficīscī, profectus sum, *to set out*
quārtus, -a, -um, *fourth*
silva, -ae, f., *woods, forest*
trādūcō, -ere, trādūxī, trāductus, *to lead across, bring across*
trānseō, trānsīre, trānsīvī or **trānsiī, trānsitus**, irreg., *to go across, cross*
ubi, conj. and adv., *where; when*
ut, conj. + subjunctive, *so that, in order that, that, to*
vērō, adv., *truly; even; in fact*

11   *pāgus, -ī, m., *community, district; clan.*
     Tigurīnus, -a, -um, Tigurinus (referring to the name of a Helvetian clan
       and, in the plural, the people of the clan).
     cīvitās, cīvitātis, f., *state, nation.*
12   quattuor pāgōs: Caesar gives the name of only one other clan, Verbigenus.
     dīvīsa: an adjective. Compare **Gallia est omnis dīvīsa.**
     cum domō exīsset: *when it* (the clan) *had left its home.*
13   memoriā: *within the memory (of)* . . . *, in the lifetime (of)* . . . *, ablative of time
       within which.*
     L. Cassius, -ī, m., *Lucius Cassius* (consul in 107 B.C.).
     interficiō, interficere, interfēcī, interfectus, to kill.
     exercitus, -ūs, m., *army.*
14   iugum, -ī, n., *yoke.*
          sub iugum: to force a Roman army **sub iugum** was symbolic of Roman
            submission to a foreign power and a stinging record of disgrace. Two
            javelins were placed at a distance from each other in the ground and a
            third was placed across the top. Roman troops were forced to give up
            their weapons and march under the javelin, hunched over.
     sīve . . . sīve, conj., *whether . . . or.*
     cāsū, adv., by chance, accidentally.
15   quae pars cīvitātis Helvētiae: *the part of the Helvetian state that* . . . , where
       the antecedent (**pars**) is contained within the relative clause itself.
     īnsignis, -is, -e, clear, distinctive, significant, historic.
     calamitās, calamitātis, f., *injury, harm; disaster, defeat.*
16   *īnferō, īnferre, intulī, illātus,* irreg., *to bring in; to inflict X* (acc.) *on Y* (dat.).
     prīnceps, prīncipis, *earliest, first.*
     persolvō, persolvere, persolvī, persolūtus, *to pay off;* with **poenās**, *to pay
       the penalty, receive punishment, suffer the consequences.*
          ea prīnceps . . . persolvit: *was the first to suffer.* . . . The word **ea** picks
            up and modifies **pars** (15), but it may be left untranslated.
     Quā in rē: *In this matter, In this way.*
     nōn sōlum . . . sed etiam, conj., not only . . . but also.
17   *iniūria, -ae, f., wrongdoing, harm, injury.*
     ulcīscor, ulcīscī, ultus sum, *to avenge.*
     quod . . . interfēcerant (19): Caesar explains why his rout of the Tigurini
       also set right certain **prīvātae iniūriae.**
     eius: i.e., Caesar's.
     socer, socerī, m., *father-in-law* .
       Caesar married his third wife, Calpurnia, in 59 B.C., and her father,
         Lucius Piso, consul in 58 B.C., was the grandson of the similarly named
         Lucius Piso, an officer in Cassius' army. See pages 6–7 for background.
     L. Pīsō, L. Pīsōnis, m., *Lucius Calpurnius Piso.*
       socerī L. Pīsōnis: the genitives are dependent on **avum** (18).
18   avus, -ī, m., *grandfather.*
          quod (17) . . . avum . . . Tigurīnī: due to ellipsis, the verb for this clause
            must be drawn from a later instance, in this case, **interfēcerant** (19).
     eōdem proeliō quō: *in the same battle (as that) in which.* . . .

A public and private injury is avenged by the surprise raid.

Is pāgus appellābātur Tigurīnus; nam omnis cīvitās Helvētia in 11
quattuor pāgōs dīvīsa est. Hic pāgus ūnus, cum domō exīsset, patrum 12
nostrōrum memoriā L. Cassium cōnsulem interfēcerat et eius exercitum 13
sub iugum mīserat. Ita sīve cāsū sīve cōnsiliō deōrum immortālium, 14
quae pars cīvitātis Helvētiae īnsignem calamitātem populō Rōmānō 15
intulerat, ea prīnceps poenās persolvit. Quā in rē Caesar nōn sōlum 16
pūblicās, sed etiam prīvātās iniūriās ultus est, quod eius socerī L. Pīsōnis 17
avum, L. Pīsōnem lēgātum, Tigurīnī eōdem proeliō quō Cassium 18
interfēcerant. 19

Caesar, *De bello Gallico* I.12

Comprehension Questions

1. How was Helvetia organized politically? (11–12)
2. What was the name of the clan decimated in the raid? What encounter had this clan had with the Romans fifty years earlier? (11–14)
3. The words **patrum nostrōrum memoriā** (12–13) reveal a living connection between the present and the past in the minds of Caesar's audience. How does Caesar use this to his advantage in disarming potential criticism of the handling or brutality of the night raid?
4. What is the significance of the phrase **sīve cāsū sīve cōnsiliō deōrum immortālium**? (14)
5. Personally and politically, what added benefit might Caesar have gained from this raid? (16–19)

VOCABULARY REVIEW

cōnsilium, -ī, n., *plan, purpose*
cōnsul, cōnsulis, m., *consul*
deus, -ī, m., *god*
domus, -ūs, abl., **domō**, f., *home*
exeō, exīre, exīvī or **exiī, exitus**, irreg., *to go out, leave*
īdem, eadem, idem, *the same*
immortālis, -is, -e, *immortal*
lēgātus, -ī, m., *envoy; legate, lieutenant*
memoria, -ae, f., *memory*
mittō, -ere, mīsī, missus, *to send*

nam, conj., *for, because*
pater, patris, m., *father*
poena, -ae, f., *penalty, punishment*
populus, -ī, m., *people, nation*
prīvātus, -a, -um, *private, personal*
pūblicus, -a, -um, *public*
quattuor, *four*
rēs, reī, f., *thing; matter; situation*
Rōmānus, -a, -um, *Roman*; m. pl., *the Romans*
sub, prep. + abl. or acc., *under, beneath*

HELVETIAN FURY AND THE GERMAN THREAT

After this battle, Caesar had a bridge built over the Saône and took his army across it so that he could pursue the remaining Helvetian troops. They were thrown into confusion by his sudden arrival—they realized that the operation of crossing the river, which they themselves had taken 20 days and a great deal of trouble to complete, he had carried out in one. They sent envoys to him led by Divico, who had been the leader of the Helvetii in the war against Cassius.

Caesar, *De bello Gallico*, I.13

Divico asked for peace. Caesar agreed, but he demanded that the Helvetii give hostages to him and restitution to the Aedui and Allobroges. Divico's response was that the Helvetii took hostages, they did not give them.

Caesar headed for Bibracte, the Aeduan capital, to secure grain for his troops. When the Helvetii learned of this, they pursued the Romans and engaged the rearguard. Caesar drew up his legion in a triple battle line on a hill and waited.

The Helvetii pursued us with all their wagons. They collected their baggage together in one place, then lining up in very close order, they drove our cavalry back, formed a phalanx, and moved up toward our front line. Caesar had all the officers' horses, beginning with his own, taken out of sight so that the danger would be the same for everyone, and no one would have any hope of escape. He encouraged his troops, then joined battle.

Because they were hurling their javelins down from the higher ground, they easily broke through the enemy's phalanx, and when that disintegrated, they charged them with drawn swords. It was a great handicap for the Gauls as they fought that several of their shields could be pierced and pinned together by a single javelin, which they could not wrench out because the iron head would bend; and with the left arm encumbered it was not possible for them to fight properly, so that many, after tugging frequently on their shield arms, preferred to let go their shields and fight unprotected. At last, exhausted by their wounds, they began to retreat, withdrawing towards a hill that was about a mile away. They gained this hill and our men were moving towards them when the Boii and the Tulingi, who, with a force of some 15,000 men, completed the enemy's column and protected their rearguard, marched up and, attacking on our exposed right flank, surrounded us.

Caesar, *De bello Gallico*, I.24–25

Caesar sent his first and second line against the Helvetii and his third line against the Boii and Tulingi. The Romans succeeded in taking the Helvetian camp and baggage train. In surrender, the Helvetii had to give up their weapons, turn over hostages and deserters to the Romans, and return to Helvetia. Of the 368,000 Helvetii who had set out, 110,000 returned alive to their homeland.

Caesar's victory over the Helvetii earned him renewed recognition from tribes all over Gaul. In a private meeting with Gallic chiefs,

the Aeduan Diviciacus, speaking on behalf of them all, told the following story. In the whole of Gaul there were two factions, one led by the Aedui, the other by the Arverni. For many years they struggled fiercely between themselves for supremacy until eventually the Arverni and the Sequani sent for German mercenaries; about 15,000 came across the Rhine in the first contingent. But after those uncivilized savages had developed a liking for the good land and the high standard of living enjoyed by the Gauls, more came across, until by now there were some 120,000 of them in Gaul.   Caesar, *De bello Gallico*, I.31

The Aedui in defeat had to turn over leading citizens to the Sequani as hostages; but worse for the Sequani, the Germans occupied a third of their land and were demanding another third for more of their countrymen.

Then too Caesar saw that it was dangerous for Rome to have the Germans gradually getting into the habit of crossing the Rhine and coming into Gaul in vast numbers. Once they had occupied the whole of Gaul he did not imagine that such a fierce uncivilized people would refrain from moving out, as the Cimbri and Teutones had done before them, into the Province and then pressing on into Italy, especially as there was only the river Rhône separating our province from the territory of the Sequani.   Caesar, *De bello Gallico*, I.33

But to an invitation from Caesar that they discuss the question of German settlement in Gaul, the German leader Ariovistus replied that to the victor go the spoils. In the meantime reports reached Caesar that recent German arrivals were ravaging Aeduan land, that one hundred more clans were awaiting transport, and, more troubling, that Ariovistus was heading toward Besancon, the capital of the Sequani and a well-stocked military stronghold. Caesar marched his troops through the night to take Besançon first and use it himself to restock and regroup. A more dangerous enemy than the Germans awaited him there.

1   **Dum ... morātur** (2): the subject is Caesar. The conjunction **dum**, meaning *while*, may be followed by the present tense even when referring to past events; the verb is best translated into English as an imperfect: *While Caesar was. . . .*

    paucōs diēs: *for a . . .* , accusative of duration of time.

    Vesontiō, Vesontiōnis, m./f., *Besançon* (the largest town of the Sequani).

      ad Vesontiōnem: generally, names of towns are put into the accusative without a preposition to indicate motion to; when **ad** is used, it has the meaning of *in the vicinity of* or *close to*.

    *****rēs frūmentāria, reī frūmentāriae**, f., *grain supply*.

    commeātus, -ūs, m., *food supply, provisions*.

      reī frūmentāriae commeātūsque: the genitives are dependent on **causā** (2), which in this context has the added meaning, *for the sake of arranging, in order to obtain*.

2   **percontātiō, percontātiōnis**, f., *inquiry, questioning*.

    ex percontātiōne . . . , tantus subitō timor . . . occupāvit (7): a clear cause and effect arises here between the questioning of Caesar's men concerning the Germans (**ex percontātiōne**) and their subsequent reaction to the answer (**tantus . . . timor**); a translation of **ex** to express this clearly might be: *as a result of* or *in response to*.

    nostrōrum: *of our men* or *from our men*, a subjective genitive expressing the source of the questioning. The possessive adjectives *****noster** and *****suus** in the plural commonly stand alone in Caesar and need the additional noun *men* or *soldiers* in your translation.

    *****vōx, vōcis**, f., *voice*; pl., *words, statements, replies*.

    vōcibus: also governed by **ex**.

3   **quī ... Germānōs ... esse praedicābant** (4): a relative clause with an embedded indirect statement: *who* (i.e., the Gauls and traders) *kept declaring that the Germans were (endowed with). . . .* The three nouns **magnitūdine, virtūte**, and **exercitātiōne** are ablatives of description.

4   **exercitātiō, exercitātiōnis**, f., *training*.

    praedicō, -āre, -āvī, -ātus, *to report, declare*.

    *****saepenumerō**, adv., *very often, frequently*.

5   **sēsē ... potuisse** (6): these are the subject accusative and infinitive of an indirect statement introduced by **dīcēbant** (6).

    *****congredior, congredī, congressus sum**, *to come into contact; to fight*.

      saepenumerō (4) **... cum hīs congressōs**: translate as a unit; the ablative **Germānīs** is understood with **hīs**.

    nē ... quidem: the words that stand within this phrase in Latin follow *not even* in English; e.g., **nē fortūna quidem**, *not even fortune*.

    aciēs, aciēī, f., *edge; stare, gaze*.

    aciem oculōrum: the idiom **nē ... quidem** extends to these words too.

7   **mediocriter**, adv., *moderately*.

    nōn mediocriter: *not moderately = strongly, deeply*. This is an example of litotes or understatement in which a positive thought is expressed by negating its opposite.

    *****perturbō, -āre, -āvī, -ātus**, *to throw into confusion; to disturb, upset*.

    ut ... perturbāret: the subject, *it*, refers to **timor**.

With a garrison in place at Besançon, Caesar makes necessary preparations,
while rumors about the Germans evoke an unexpected reaction from among the
Roman legions.

39. Dum paucōs diēs ad Vesontiōnem reī frūmentāriae commeātūsque   1
causā morātur, ex percontātiōne nostrōrum vōcibusque Gallōrum ac   2
mercātōrum, quī ingentī magnitūdine corporum Germānōs, incrēdibilī   3
virtūte atque exercitātiōne in armīs esse praedicābant (saepenumerō   4
sēsē cum hīs congressōs nē vultum quidem atque aciem oculōrum   5
dīcēbant ferre potuisse), tantus subitō timor omnem exercitum   6
occupāvit ut nōn mediocriter omnium mentēs animōsque perturbāret.   7

Comprehension Questions

1. With leisure time on their hands, what seemingly innocent questions were the Romans asking and of whom? (2–3)
2. What three characteristics of the Germans were singled out? (3–4)
3. How did the Gallic traders and merchants vouch for the authority of their observations? (4–6)
4. Lines 1–7 are one sentence. How does Caesar effectively create suspense in revealing the reaction of his men to the rumors?
5. Examine Caesar's choice of words in lines 6–7 (**tantus . . . perturbāret**) and explain how, behind the simplicity of the clause, there are patterns of sound and meaning that help convey the extent of the fear gripping his men.
6. Why is the general truth that a soldier has three enemies—boredom, imagination, and the enemy—an apt assessment of the situation?

VOCABULARY REVIEW

arma, -ōrum, n. pl., *arms, weapons*
causā, prep. + preceding gen., *for the sake of*
corpus, corporis, n., *body*
dīcō, -ere, dīxī, dictus, *to say*
diēs, -ēī, m., *day*
dum, conj., *while*
ferō, ferre, tulī, lātus, irreg., *to bring; to bear, endure*
ingēns, ingentis, *big, huge*
magnitūdō, magnitūdinis, f., *greatness, size*
mēns, mentis, mentium, f., *mind*
moror, -ārī, morātus sum, *to remain, stay*
nē . . . quidem, idiom, *not even*
occupō, -āre, -āvī, -ātus, *to seize*
paucī, -ae, -a, *a few*
subitō, adv., *suddenly*
tantus, -a, -um, *such, so great*
timor, timōris, m., *fear, panic*
vultus, -ūs, m., *face; expression*

8   **Hic**: i.e., **timor** (6).
     ā: *with.*
    *tribūnus mīlitum, tribūnī mīlitum, m., *military tribune.*
    praefectus, -ī, m., *officer; commander of the auxilaries.*
    reliquīsque: *and the others.*
      tribūnīs mīlitum, praefectīs reliquīsque: referring to individuals with
        little if any experience of frontline battle, who may have accompanied
        Caesar with an eye to improving their political and financial standing,
        an arrangement that is broadly implied in the word **amīcitia** (9). The
        tribūnī mīlitum were assigned to the legion and usually had non-
        combat assignments, such as leading troops on a march or handling
        watch patrols. Although **tribūnī mīlitum** were in earlier times
        responsible for leadership in battle, Caesar shifted this responsibility to
        legates and quaestors, who were his appointments. The **praefectī** refer
        to the officers of those auxilaries that consisted of archers and slingers.

9   **ex urbe**: i.e., Rome.
    nōn magnum: *not much, very little.* See page 14, note to line 7 for litotes.
    rēs mīlitāris, reī mīlitāris, f., *military affairs.*

10   ***ūsus, -ūs**, m., *use; practice, experience.*
    quōrum alius aliā causā illātā: *each one of them, introducing a different*
      reason. . . . ; lit., *of which (one with one reason brought,) another with an another*
      reason brought. The first half of an **alius . . . alius** expression is left out
      when **alius** is repeated in another case (here, **alius aliā**).
    quam . . . dīceret (11): *which (each) said. . . .*
    ad proficīscendum (11): *to . . . ,* gerund with **ad** to express purpose.

11   **necessāriam**: supply **causam**.
    ut . . . licēret (12): supply **sibi**.
    eius: i.e., Caesar's.
    voluntās, voluntātis, f., *will; appproval, permission.*

12   ***pudor, pudōris**, m., *shame; sense of honor; feeling of dishonor.*
    addūcō, addūcere, addūxī, adductus, *to lead; to sway, influence.*

13   **fingō, fingere, fīnxī, fīctus**, *to form, shape; to control.*
    vultum fingere, *to control one's expression; to maintain a calm exterior.*
    interdum, adv., *sometimes, at times.*

14   **tabernāculum, -ī**, n., *tent.*

15   **queror, querī, questus sum**, *to complain about, grumble about.*
    familiāris, familiāris, familiārium, m., *companion, close friend.*

16   **miseror, miserārī, miserātus sum**, *to bemoan, bewail, cry over.*
    *vulgō, adv., *everywhere.*
    tōtīs castrīs: = in **tōtīs castrīs** or per **tōta castra**. The preposition **in** is
      often omitted when ablatives of place are modified by **tōtus** or **omnis**.
    testāmentum, -ī, n., *will* (as in last will and testament).
    obsignō, -āre, -āvī, -ātus, *to sign and seal.*

18   **mīlitēs centuriōnēsque quīque**: the use of more conjunctions than is
      needed is called polysyndeton.
    *equitātus, -ūs, m., *cavalry.*
    *praesum, praeesse, praefuī, irreg. + dat., *to be in command (of).*
      quīque equitātuī praeerant: = et eī, quī equitātuī praeerant.

Panic begins to spread throughout the Roman camp.

    Hic prīmum ortus est ā tribūnīs mīlitum, praefectīs, reliquīsque quī 8
ex urbe amīcitiae causā Caesarem secūtī nōn magnum in rē mīlitārī 9
ūsum habēbant: quōrum alius aliā causā illātā, quam sibi ad 10
proficīscendum necessāriam esse dīceret, petēbat ut eius voluntāte 11
discēdere licēret; nōnnūllī pudōre adductī, ut timōris suspīciōnem 12
vītārent, remanēbant. Hī neque vultum fingere neque interdum 13
lacrimās tenēre poterant; abditī in tabernāculīs aut suum fātum 14
querēbantur aut cum familiāribus suīs commūne perīculum 15
miserābantur. Vulgō tōtīs castrīs testāmenta obsignābantur. Hōrum 16
vōcibus ac timōre paulātim etiam eī, quī magnum in castrīs ūsum 17
habēbant, mīlitēs centuriōnēsque quīque equitātuī praeerant, 18
perturbābantur. 19

Comprehension Questions

1. Lines 8–16 are Caesar's judgment of non-legionary soldiers in a war setting. Initially, of what inexcusable behavior were they guilty? (8–12) Why were some of these men staying rather than looking for reasons to leave? (12–13) Why would their subsequent behavior (13–16) still leave them open to charges of cowardice?
2. Who were finally becoming unnerved by the spreading rumors and panic? Why would their alarm have been more of a problem for Caesar? (16–19)

VOCABULARY REVIEW

alius . . . alius, *one . . . another*
amīcitia, -ae, f., *friendship*
centuriō, centuriōnis, m., *centurion*
commūnis, -is, -e, *common*
discēdō, -ere, discessī, discessūrus, *to leave, go away*
etiam, adv., *also, even*
fātum, -ī, n., *fate*
habeō, -ēre, -uī, -itus, *to have*
īnferrō, īnferre, intulī, illātus, irreg. verb, *to bring*
lacrima, -ae, f., *tear*
licet, -ēre, licuit + dat., *it is permitted* or *allowed*
mīles, mīlitis, m., *soldier*
necessārius, -a, -um, *necessary*
neque . . . neque, conj., *neither . . . nor*

nōnnūllī, -ae, -a, *some*
orior, -īrī, ortus sum, *to rise, arise, begin*
paulātim, adv., *gradually*
perīculum, -ī, n., *danger*
petō, -ere, petīvī, petītus, *to seek; to ask*
prīmum, adv., *first*
remaneō, -ēre, remānsī, *to remain, stay behind*
sequor, -ī, secūtus sum, *to follow*
suspīciō, suspīciōnis, f., *suspicion*
teneō, -ēre, tenuī, tentus, *to hold*
tōtus, -a, -um, *whole, entire*
urbs, urbis, f., *city*
vītō, -āre, -āvī, -ātus, *to avoid*

20   **Quī sē ex hīs . . . volēbant, . . . dīcēbant** (23): *(Some) of these* (**ex hīs**), *who wished . . . , kept saying that. . . .* , referring to the last group of soldiers and officers (16–19), who will now claim that there are legitimate reasons for their nervousness.

    *exīstimō, -āre, -āvī, -ātus, *to think, believe, judge, consider.*

    nōn sē . . . verērī (21): what are the three objects of **verērī**?

21   ***angustiae, -ārum,** f. pl., *narrowness; difficulties.*

22   **intercēdō, intercēdere, intercessī, intercessūrus,** *to lie* or *be between.*

    quae intercēderent: subordinate clauses within an indirect statement take a subjunctive; in translation the subjunctive will generally become an indicative of the same tense.

    *Ariovistus, -ī, m.; *Ariovistus* (leader of the German tribes).

    aut rem frūmentāriam, ut . . . posset, timēre (23): with verbs of fearing, **nē** means *that* and **ut** means *that . . . not.* Although the accusative **rem frūmentāriam** is the object of **timēre**, translate it as if it were the subject of **posset:** *or (that) they were afraid that the grain supply could not.* . . .

23   ***commodē,** adv., *adequately, suitably.*

    supportō, -āre, -āvī, -ātus, *to bring up; to provide, supply.*

24   ***signum, -ī,** n., *sign, signal; military standard.*

    cum castra movērī ac signa ferrī iussisset: the two military idioms, ***castra movēre,** *to break camp* and ***signa ferre,** *to advance* (lit., *to bring the standards),* are put in the passive to convey in an absolute sense the idea of breaking camp and advancing. Caesar is the subject of **iussisset,** which represents a future perfect indicative in direct speech.

    *fore: alternate form of **futūrōs esse.** From what verbs and what tense are **fore** here and **lātūrōs (esse)** in line 25? You will find that **esse** is often omitted from the perfect passive and future active infinitives.

25   ***dictō audiēns, dictō audientis,** *obedient;* lit., *listening to the word* (= the order).

26   **Haec:** sometimes in Latin a word is pulled out of a clause for the purpose of emphasis and continuity with preceding events; the demonstrative **haec,** referring to the events of the previous paragraph, belongs in the **cum** clause as the object of **animadvertisset.** Caesar is the subject of the verb.

    cōnsiliō . . . cōnsilium (27): in these two instances **cōnsilium** means *meeting* but in line 28 it means *plan* or *purpose.*

27   ***ōrdō, ōrdinis,** m., *rank.*

    adhibeō, -ēre, -uī, -itus, *to bring in; to summon.*

    convocātō cōnsiliō omniumque ōrdinum . . . adhibitīs centuriōnibus: unlike a council of war, to which only officers and the six centurions of the first cohort of each legion were invited, Caesar is calling an emergency meeting that includes all the centurions in the camp.

28   **incūsō, -āre, -āvī, -ātus,** *to reprimand, rebuke.*

    prīmum, quod . . . putārent (29): *first, because they thought.* . . . , a causal clause with subjunctive since the reason belongs to the troops not Caesar.

    quam in partem: *in what direction.*

29   **sibi quaerendum aut cōgitandum:** supply **esse** to complete the passive periphrastic: *(that) it was their business to . . .* ; lit., *(that) it was necessary for them to.* . . .

Hearing various reasons and excuses for the skittishness in the camp and warned of a mutiny, Caesar responds quickly.

Quī sē ex hīs minus timidōs exīstimārī volēbant, nōn sē hostem   20
verērī, sed angustiās itineris et magnitūdinem silvārum, quae   21
intercēderent inter ipsōs atque Ariovistum, aut rem frūmentāriam, ut   22
satis commodē supportārī posset, timēre dīcēbant. Nōnnūllī etiam   23
Caesarī nūntiābant, cum castra movērī ac signa ferrī iussisset, nōn fore   24
dictō audientēs mīlitēs neque propter timōrem signa lātūrōs.   25
40. Haec cum animadvertisset, convocātō cōnsiliō omniumque   26
ōrdinum ad id cōnsilium adhibitīs centuriōnibus, vehementer eōs   27
incūsāvit: prīmum, quod aut quam in partem aut quō cōnsiliō   28
dūcerentur sibi quaerendum aut cōgitandum putārent.   29

Comprehension Questions

1. Look closely at lines 1–19 on pages 15 and 17. Point out words for fearing based on **timēre**. As Caesar's most capable soldiers try to disown their fears, how does Caesar let us see through their pretense by introducing the verb **verērī** (21) to contrast with **timēre** (23)?
2. A greater concern has reached Caesar in lines 23–25. What is it?
3. Why has Caesar invited all the centurions to the meeting? (26–27)
4. Speaking to the essence of leadership, over what two areas did Caesar challenge his men for presuming to question his authority? (28–29)

VOCABULARY REVIEW

animadvertō, -ere, animadvertī, animadversus, *to notice*
aut, conj., *or*
cōgitō, -āre, -āvī, -ātus, *to think, consider*
convocō, -āre, -āvī, -ātus, *to call together, convene*
dūcō, -ere, dūxī, ductus, *to lead*
hostis, hostis, hostium, m., *an enemy,* m. pl., *the enemy*
iter, itineris, n., *route; march*
iubeō, -ēre, iussī, iussus, *to order*
minus, adv., *less*
moveō, -ēre, mōvī, mōtus, *to move*
neque, conj., *nor, and . . . not*
nūntiō, -āre, -āvī, -ātus, *to* *announce, report*
propter, prep. + acc., *because of*
putō, -āre, -āvī, -ātus, *to think*
quaerō, -ere, quaesīvī, quaesītus, *to seek; to ask*
satis, noun or adv., *enough*
sed, conj., *but*
sī, conj., *if*
timeō, -ēre, timuī, *to be afraid*
timidus, -a, -um, *fearful, cowardly*
vehementer, adv., *vigorously, strongly*
vereor, -ērī, veritus sum, *to stand in awe of; to fear*
volō, velle, voluī, irreg., *to wish, want*

30   **Ariovistum**: the remainder of Caesar's address, lines 30–69, is an extended indirect statement. Often in *De bello Gallico* indirect statement gives a summary and selective recollection of what has been said. Either use quotes and treat this speech as one coming from Caesar, in which case Caesar will use the first person for himself and the second person for his men (even though he uses the third person to refer to himself and his men in the speech) or introduce the indirect statement with what is understood in Latin, *He told them that . . .*, and then translate accordingly. In direct statement the first sentence would read: **Ariovistus, mē cōnsule, cupidissimē populī Rōmānī amīcitiam appetiit; cūr hunc tam temere quisquam ab officiō discessūrum iūdicet?**

    sē cōnsule: *during his consulship* (in direct statement: *during my consulship*). Caesar was consul in the previous year.

    *****cupidus, -a, -um**, *desirous, eager.*

31   **appetō, appetere, appetīvī** or **appetiī, appetītus**, *to seek, pursue.*

    appetīsse: = **appetīvisse.**

    hunc: i.e., Ariovistus.

    temere, adv., *recklessly, rashly.*

    quisquam, quicquam, *anyone, anything.*

    cūr . . . quisquam . . . iūdicāret (32): *why should anyone suppose that.* . . .

    *****officium, -ī**, n., *duty, task, mission.*

    discessūrum: what has been omitted from this verb form? See page 18, note to line 24 for the general rule. Here, *depart from = give up on.*

32   **Sibi quidem persuādērī** (32): *It was persuaded to him* (Caesar) *at any rate (that).* . . . = *He at any rate was convinced (that).* . . .

    postulātum, -ī, n., *demand, request.*

33   **aequitās, aequitātis,** f., *fairness.*

    *****condiciō, condiciōnis**, f., *condition, agreement, terms.*

    *****perspiciō, perspicere, perspexī, perspectus**, *to look closely; to see clearly.*

    cognitīs suīs postulātīs atque aequitāte condiciōnum perspectā: *once his* (Caesar's) *requests were.* . . . (chiasmus). The audience is reminded that Ariovistus had received a fair offer of reconciliation from Caesar that should make him reconsider the prospect of losing Roman goodwill.

    eum: i.e., Ariovistus, subject of **repudiātūrum** (34).

    suam: what noun is understood by ellipsis?

34   **grātia, -ae**, f., *favor, goodwill.*

    repudiō, -āre, -āvī, -ātus, *to reject, turn down.*

    *****quod sī**, *but if.*

    furor, furōris, m., *frenzy, madness.*

    āmentia, -ae, f., *insanity.*

    impellō, impellere, impulī, impulsus, *to urge on, drive.*

35   **bellum īnferre**, idiom, *to wage war.*

    bellum intulisset: *he* (Ariovistus) *were to wage war.*

    tandem, adv., *finally;* for emphasis, *really, in the world, on earth.*

    dē suā . . . aut dē ipsīus . . . (36): the reflexive **suā** refers to Caesar's men, the intensive **ipsīus** to Caesar, *of their own . . . or of his.* . . .

36   *****dēspērō, -āre, -āvī, -ātus** + **dē** + abl., *to lose hope of, give up on.*

Caesar tells his men why Ariovistus will not seek war.

    Ariovistum sē cōnsule cupidissimē populī Rōmānī amīcitiam   **30**
appetīsse; cūr hunc tam temere quisquam ab officiō discessūrum   **31**
iūdicāret? Sibi quidem persuādērī cognitīs suīs postulātīs atque   **32**
aequitāte condiciōnum perspectā eum neque suam neque populī   **33**
Rōmānī grātiam repudiātūrum. Quod sī furōre atque āmentiā impulsus   **34**
bellum intulisset, quid tandem verērentur? Aut cūr dē suā virtūte aut   **35**
dē ipsīus dīligentiā dēspērārent?   **36**

Comprehension Questions

1. **Amīcitia populī Rōmānī** guaranteed Roman support and favored status to
   a foreign ally; Ariovistus had received that honor in the previous year,
   probably at the urging of the then consul, Caesar. What slant does the
   superlative **cupidissimē** give to Caesar's account of the deal? (30–31)
2. How might Caesar have characterized any leader—in this case, Ariovistus—who rejected an offer of fair Roman treatment? (31–35)
3. On the following pages consider the equation that Caesar insinuates here,
   that Roman **virtūs** and **dīligentia** overcome enemy **furor** and **āmentia**.
   What is Caesar's purpose in developing this equation?

VOCABULARY REVIEW
---

cognōscō, -ere, cognōvī,
  cognitus, *to find out, learn*
cūr, adv., *why*
dīligentia, -ae, f., *diligence,*
  thoroughness
persuādeō, -ēre, persuāsī,

persuāsus + dat., *to persuade,*
  convince
quidem, adv., *certainly, at any rate*
quis, quid, *who, what*
tam, adv., *so*

Coin of the emperor Galba addressing his troops

37   **Factum eius hostis perīculum**: supply **esse** and translate: *(He said that) a test* (**perīculum**) *had been made of this enemy.*

     memoriā: for the expression, see page 10, note to line 13.

38   **Cimbrī, -ōrum**, m. pl., *the Cimbri.*

     Teutonī, -ōrum or **Teutonēs, Teutonum**, m. pl., *the Teutones.*

     Gaius Marius, -ī, m., *Gaius Marius.*

     *****pellō, pellere, pepulī, pulsus**, *to drive back; to rout.*

       Cimbrīs et Teutonīs ā Gaiō Mariō pulsīs: what construction? Experiment with several different translations.

       cum (37) . . . exercitus . . . vidēbātur (39): *(on the occasion) when the (Roman) army was seen. . . .* Apparently, the indicative **vidēbātur** is carried over from direct speech to stress the temporal nature of the event without suggesting that the battle had been fought for certain motives, as a subjunctive here might have suggested.

       nōn minōrem laudem . . . quam (39): *no less acclaim than = just as much acclaim as,* object of **meritus (39)** and an example of litotes.

39   *****imperātor, imperātōris**, m., *commander, general.*

     mereor, merērī, meritus sum, *to deserve, earn.*

       meritus: supply **esse**. The infinitive depends on **vidēbātur**; the nominative **meritus** may be used since it modifies the subject of the verb on which it depends.

       factum: a word repeated from line 37: *there had been (a test) made.*

40   **servīlis, -is, -e**, *involving slaves.*

       servīlī tumultū: = **tumultū servōrum**: *during . . . ,* abl. of time when. Among the slaves that joined the slave revolts led by Spartacus in 73–71 B.C. were many of German and Gallic origin, including Cimbri and Teutones captured by Marius years earlier.

       quōs tamen: *whom nevertheless = even though . . . them.* The antecedent is the slaves implied in the adjective **servīlis**.

     aliquid, adv., *somewhat, to some extent.*

     disciplīna, -ae, f., *instruction, training.*

       quam: although singular under the influence of the immediate antecedent **disciplīna**, the relative refers to both **ūsus** and **disciplīna**.

41   **sublevō, -āre, -āvī, -ātus**, *to lift up; to help, aid.*

       Ex quō iūdicārī posse quantum . . . bonī (42): *From which it can be judged how much of an advantage* (lit., *how much of good*).

42   **cōnstantia, -ae**, f., *firmness, steadfastness.*

       quōs . . . timuissent, hōs posteā . . . superāssent (43): *these (slaves,* **hōs**), *whom they* (the Romans) *. . . , they later. . . .* Caesar makes his point sharper by withholding the antecedent until after the relative clause.

     aliquamdiū, adv., *for some time, for a long time.*

     inermis, -is, -e, *unarmed.*

       inermēs: modifying **quōs**.

43   **victor, victōris**, m., *conqueror;* with adjectival force, *victorious.*

       armātōs ac victōrēs: modifying **hōs**, with concessive force: *although the slaves were. . . .*

     superāssent: contracted from **superāvissent**.

*His men are reminded that twice in the not so distant past Roman troops had
defeated an enemy equal in stature to the Germans.*

Factum eius hostis perīculum patrum nostrōrum memoriā, cum, 37
Cimbrīs et Teutonīs ā Gaiō Mariō pulsīs, nōn minōrem laudem exercitus 38
quam ipse imperātor meritus vidēbātur; factum etiam nūper in Italiā 39
servīlī tumultū, quōs tamen aliquid ūsus ac disciplīna, quam ā nōbīs 40
accēpissent, sublevārent. Ex quō iūdicārī posse quantum habēret in sē 41
bonī cōnstantia, proptereā quod, quōs aliquamdiū inermēs sine causā 42
timuissent, hōs posteā armātōs ac victōrēs superāssent. 43

Comprehension Questions

1. All Romans had heard of the spectacular victories of the Roman legions
   under Gaius Marius over the marauding German invaders from the north,
   the Cimbri and Teutones, in 102–101 B.C. (see pages 6–7). Why does Caesar
   allude to that here? (37–39) What similarities might Caesar have hoped his
   audience would see between then and now, between Marius and Caesar?
2. The Slave Wars of 73–71 B.C. constituted an equally serious threat to the
   security of Rome, this time from within Italy. In fact, many in Caesar's
   audience had participated in these wars. Drawing on the same image of an
   undisciplined but physically powerful enemy, how does Caesar hope to use
   this allusion to dispel the current fear of the Germans?

VOCABULARY REVIEW

accipiō, -ere, accēpī, acceptus, *to
   get, receive*
armātus, -a, -um, *armed*
bonus, -a, -um, *good*
Italia, -ae, f., *Italy*
laus, laudis, f., *praise, acclaim*
minor, minor, minus, gen.,
   minōris, *smaller; less*
nōs, *we; us*
nūper, adv., *recently*
posteā, adv., *afterwards, later*

quam, conj., in comparisons, *than*
quantus, -a, -um, *how great, how
   much*
sine, prep. + abl., *without*
superō, -āre, -āvī, -ātus, *to be
   superior; to defeat, conquer*
tamen, adv., *however, nevertheless*
tumultus, -ūs, m., *uproar,
   commotion; uprising*
videō, -ēre, vīdī, vīsus, *to see*

44 Dēnique hōs esse: *Finally, (he said that) these were.* . . .
46 *plērumque, adv., *generally, usually; often.*
    superārint: contracted from superāverint.
    quī tamen: *and yet these (Helvetii).*
47 quōs: *any (one of his soldiers).* After sī, nisi, num, or nē, the indefinite
    pronoun quis, quid or adjective *quī, qua, quod means *any(one).*
    adversus, -a, -um, *unfavorable, unsuccessful.*
        adversum proelium: *unsuccessful battle = defeat.* This and the fuga
            Gallōrum, both subjects of commovēret, refer to the battle of Ad-
            magetobriga in 61 B.C., when the Gauls were defeated by Ariovistus.
48 hōs: *these (same individuals),* corresponding to sī quōs in the line above.
    *reperiō, reperīre, repperī, repertus, *to find, discover.*
    diūturnitās, diūturnitātis, f., *duration, length.*
        diūturnitāte bellī: *due to* . . . , ablative of cause with dēfatīgātīs.
    *dēfatīgō, -āre, -āvī, -ātus, *to wear out, exhaust.*
        dēfatīgātīs Gallīs Ariovistum . . . subitō adortum . . . vīcisse (51): *(that)*
        since the Gauls were exhausted . . . , *Ariovistus* . . . *suddenly attacked* (lit.,
        having attacked) and defeated (them). Dēspērantēs and dispersōs,
        modifying eōs understood, are the real objects of vīcisse.
49 palūs, palūdis, f., *swamp, marsh.*
    castrīs sē ac palūdibus tenuisset: *he had kept himself* (safely protected) *by
        means of.* . . . Marshes surrounded the German camp.
50 potestās, potestātis, f., *power; possibility, opportunity.*
    neque (49) suī potestātem fēcisset: *and he had not made an opportunity of
        himself,* more fully, *and he had not given them a chance to fight him.*
    dispergō, dispergere, dispersī, dispersus, *to disperse, scatter, split up.*
51 *ratiō, ratiōnis, f., *reason; plan; method; stratagem, ploy.*
        magis ratiōne et cōnsiliō quam virtūte: the real source, according to
        Caesar, of Ariovistus' victory: *more by means of* . . . *than.* . . .
        Cui ratiōnī . . . locus fuisset, hāc nē ipsum quidem . . . posse (53): *For
        which ploy there had been an opportunity* . . . , *by this (same ploy) not even
        (Ariovistus) himself could.* . . . , or *By this ploy, for which.* . . .
52 *barbarus, -a, -um, *foreign; uncivilized, undisciplined.*
    imperītus, -a, -um, *inexperienced.*
53 capī: present infinitive for the future: *would be taken (by surprise).*
54 Quī . . . , facere (55): *(As for those) who* . . . , *they were acting.*
    simulātiō, simulātiōnis, f., *pretending, pretense.*
        simulātiōnem: *a pretense of (concern for)* + gen.
55 cōnferō, cōnferre, contulī, collātus, irreg., *to bring together; to assign;* + in
    + acc., *to shift X onto Y.*
56 praescrībō, praescrībere, praescrīpsī, praescrīptus, *to give orders.*
    Haec sibi esse cūrae: double dative: *These (matters) were his concern.*
        Two other double datives you will meet in Caesar are esse praesidiō +
        dat., *to protect someone* and esse subsidiō + dat., *to help someone.*
    *frūmentum, -ī, n., *grain* (i.e., cut grain); pl., *crops* (i.e., grain in the fields).
57 Sēquanōs, Leucōs, Lingonēs: names of Gallic tribes.
    sumministrō, -āre, -āvī, -ātus, *to supply, provide.*
58 ipsōs . . . iūdicātūrōs: *they* (his men) *would themselves decide.*

More recently, Caesar recalls, the Helvetii have beaten the Germans.

Dēnique hōs esse eōsdem Germānōs quibuscum saepenumerō 44
Helvētiī congressī nōn sōlum in suīs sed etiam in illōrum fīnibus 45
plērumque superārint, quī tamen parēs esse nostrō exercituī nōn 46
potuerint. Sī quōs adversum proelium et fuga Gallōrum commovēret, 47
hōs, sī quaererent, reperīre posse diūturnitāte bellī dēfatīgātīs Gallīs 48
Ariovistum, cum multōs mēnsēs castrīs sē ac palūdibus tenuisset neque 49
suī potestātem fēcisset, dēspērantēs iam dē pugnā et dispersōs subitō 50
adortum magis ratiōne et cōnsiliō quam virtūte vīcisse. Cui ratiōnī 51
contrā hominēs barbarōs atque imperītōs locus fuisset, hāc nē ipsum 52
quidem spērāre nostrōs exercitūs capī posse. 53
Quī suum timōrem in reī frūmentāriae simulātiōnem angustiāsque 54
itineris cōnferrent, facere arroganter, cum aut dē officiō imperātōris 55
dēspērāre aut praescrībere vidērentur. Haec sibi esse cūrae; frūmentum 56
Sēquanōs, Leucōs, Lingonēs sumministrāre, iamque esse in agrīs 57
frūmenta mātūra; dē itinere ipsōs brevī tempore iūdicātūrōs. 58

Comprehension Questions

1. Building on a logic similar to lines 37–43 but alluding to more recent events, what are Caesar's two points about the Gallo-German conflicts? (44–53)
2. In summary, how has Caesar attempted to restore Roman confidence in their fighting prowess and diminish the rumored stature of the barbaric enemy in lines 37–53?
3. Caesar decisively cuts short any discussion of his preparedness and authority to lead in lines 54–58. What does he make clear to his leading officers in these lines?

VOCABULARY REVIEW

adorior, -īrī, adortus sum, *to attack*
ager, agrī, m., *field*
arroganter, adv., *arrogantly, presumptuously*
brevis, -is, -e, *short*
capiō, -ere, cēpī, captus, *to take, capture, catch*
commoveō, -ēre, commōvī, commōtus, *to move; to alarm, upset, cause X to worry*
contrā, prep. + acc., *against*
cūra, -ae, f., *care, concern*
dēnique, adv., *finally*

homō, hominis, m., *man, person*
ille, illa, illud, *that*
locus, -ī, m., n. in pl., *place, area, location; opportunity*
magis, adv., *more*
matūrus, -a, -um, *ripe, full-grown*
mēnsis, mēnsis, m., *month*
multī, -ae, -a, *many*
pār, paris, *equal*
pugna, -ae, f., *fight, battle*
spērō, -āre, -āvī, -ātus, *to hope*
tempus, temporis, n., *time*
vincō, -ere, vīcī, victus, *to conquer, defeat*

59 **Quod ... dīcantur:** *With regard to the report that the soldiers. . . . ;* lit., *As to the fact that they* (the soldiers) *were said. . . .*
audientēs ... lātūrī: for the nominative, see page 22, note to line 39.
*__*nihil,__* adv., *not at all.*
   nihil sē eā rē commovērī: scīre enim (60): Caesar, using the reflexive **sē**, is the subject of **commovērī** and **scīre** (60): *(he said that) he was not at all worried about this matter: for he knew (that). . . .*
60 **quīcumque, quaecumque, quodcumque,** *whoever, whatever.*
   quibuscumque: dative with **dictō audiēns**, referring to leaders who had not earned the respect of their soldiers for the reasons given in lines 61–62; the antecedent, **eīs**, is understood and goes with **dēfuisse** (61).
61 **fuerit:** perfect subjunctive.
male rē gestā: *because the campaign was handled poorly,* the first of two ablatives absolute pinpointing the cause of each failure in leadership.
*__*dēsum, dēesse, dēfuī,__* irreg. + dat., *to be lacking, fall short, fail.*
facinus, facinoris, n., *action; misdeed, crime.*
comperiō, comperīre, comperī, compertus, *to discover, uncover.*
62 **avāritia, -ae,** f., *greed.*
convincō, convincere, convīcī, convictus, *to prove, clearly demonstrate.*
innocentia, -ae, f., *innocence; integrity.*
perpetuus, -a, -um, *whole, entire.*
   perpetuā vītā: = **per perpetuam vītam.**
fēlīcitās, fēlīcitātis, f., *success, good fortune.*
   Suam innocentiam ... , fēlīcitātem. ...: also governed by **scīre** (60): *(He said that he also knew) that his integrity ... , (and) that his good fortune. ...* Note how the chiasmus (an abba pattern) in lines 61–63 gives a rhetorical flourish to Caesar's line of argument: **fortūnam** (a) ... **avāritiam** (b) ... **innocentiam** (b) ... **fēlīcitātem** (a).
63 **Helvētiōrum bellō:** equivalent in thought to **in bellō contrā Helvētiōs,** ablative of time when or ablative of means.
64 **sē, quod ... , repraesentātūrum:** *(he said that) he would do at once what. . . .* When the antecedent **id** is understood, often **quod** = *what.*
longiōrem: *later.*
cōnferō, cōnferre, contulī, collātus, irreg. + **in** + acc., *to put off until.*
   collātūrus fuisset: the future participle with **esse** forms an active periphrastic: *he had been about to. . . . , he had intended to. . . .*
repraesentō, -āre, -āvī, -ātus, *to do at once.*
65 **proximā nocte:** *tonight;* lit., *on the next (= this coming) night.*
quam prīmum, idiom, *as soon as possible.*
67 **praetereā nēmō:** *no one else.*
68 **dubitō, -āre, -āvī, -ātus,** *to be uncertain, have doubts.*
eam: *it* (referring to the 10th legion).
praetōria cohors, praetōriae cohortis, f., *military bodyguard.*
70 **Huic legiōnī ... maximē** (71): this sentence stands outside the speech.
indulgeō, indulgēre, indulsī + dat., *to favor.*
71 **praecipuē,** adv., *especially.*
*__*cōnfīdō, cōnfīdere, cōnfīsus sum,__* *to be confident;* + dat., *to trust, have faith in.*

*Insofar as insubordination can be traced to poor or corrupt leadership, Caesar's
record is clean. Therefore, he will change his plans to test his men.*

Quod nōn fore dictō audientēs neque signa lātūrī dīcantur, nihil sē   59
eā rē commovērī: scīre enim, quibuscumque exercitus dictō audiēns nōn   60
fuerit, aut male rē gestā fortūnam dēfuisse aut aliquō facinore compertō   61
avāritiam esse convictam. Suam innocentiam perpetuā vītā, fēlīcitātem   62
Helvētiōrum bellō esse perspectam.   63

Itaque sē, quod in longiōrem diem collātūrus fuisset, repraesentātūrum et proximā nocte dē quārtā vigiliā castra mōtūrum, ut quam   64
sentātūrum et proximā nocte dē quārtā vigiliā castra mōtūrum, ut quam   65
prīmum intellegere posset utrum apud eōs pudor atque officium an   66
timor plūs valēret. Quod sī praetereā nēmō sequātur, tamen sē cum sōlā   67
decimā legiōne itūrum, dē quā nōn dubitet, sibique eam praetōriam   68
cohortem futūram.   69

Huic legiōnī Caesar et indulserat praecipuē et propter virtūtem   70
cōnfīdēbat maximē.   71

Caesar, *De bello Gallico* I.39–40

Comprehension Questions

1. Under what two sets of circumstances would Caesar expect to see insubordination? Why should he be spared it as a commander? What hidden promise is contained in the word **fēlīcitātem**? (59–63)
2. How did Caesar plan to force the issue of loyalty and obedience? (64–67)
3. Caesar held the 10th legion and its legate Labienus in the highest esteem. In saving his most powerful pronouncement until the end, what appointment did he give the 10th legion and what reaction to this news would he have expected and hoped for from the other legions? (67–69)

VOCABULARY REVIEW

aliquī, -ae, -a, *some* (or other)
apud, prep. + acc., *at the house of; among*
decimus, -a, -um, *tenth*
enim, postpositive conj., *for*
eō, īre, īvī or iī, itūrus, irreg., *to go*
et . . . et, conj., *both . . . and*
fortūna, -ae, f., *fortune*
intellegō, -ere, intellēxī, intellēctus, *to understand; to find out, learn*
itaque, adv., *and so, therefore*

male, adv., *badly, poorly*
maximē, adv., *very much, especially*
nēmō, nēminis, m., *no one*
nox, noctis, noctium, f., *night*
plūs, adv., *more*
praetereā, adv., *besides, moreover*
sciō, -īre, scīvī, scītus, *to know*
sōlus, -a, -um, *only, alone*
utrum . . . an, conj., *whether . . . or*
valeō, -ēre, valuī, valitūrus, *to be strong*
vīta, -ae, f., *life*

1   **Postrīdiē eius diēī**: *On the following day*; lit., *On the after-day of this day.*
   ***praesidium, -ī**, n., *guard.*
       praesidiō: *as . . .* , dative of purpose.
       quod . . . vīsum est (2): object of **relīquit**; for **quod**, see page 26, note to
           line 64. The passive **vidērī** often means *to seem* or *appear*, as here.
       satis: *(a large) enough (garrison).*
2   ***ālāriī, -ōrum**, m. pl., *auxiliary troops* (lightly armed soldiers).
   ***cōnspectus, -ūs**, m., *sight, general view.*
3   ***cōnstituō, cōnstituere, cōnstituī, cōnstitūtus**, *to set up, arrange, place.*
       minus multitūdine . . . valēbat (4): *he was weaker in the number (of) . . .* ; lit.,
           he was less strong in respect to the number (of). . . .
   ***legiōnārius, -a, -um**, *of the legion, legionary.*
4   **prō**: *in comparison with, compared to.*
   ***speciēs, -ēī**, f., *sight; appearance.*
       ad speciem: *for appearances' sake, to give the impression of strength.*
   ***ūtor, ūtī, ūsus sum** + abl., *to use, employ.*
       ipse: *Caesar, in person,* a frequent use of **ipse**.
       triplex, triplicis, *triple.*
5   ***īnstruō, īnstruere, īnstrūxī, īnstrūctus**, *to build;* of troops, *to draw up, form.*
   ***aciēs, -ēī**, f., *battle line.*
       triplicī īnstrūctā aciē: the triple battle line was a standard formation.
   ***usque ad** + acc., *as far as, right up to.*
   ***dēmum**, adv., *finally, at last.*
   ***necessāriō**, adv., *perforce, by necessity.*
6   **castrīs**: *out of . . .* , ablative, influenced by the **ē** (for **ex**) in **ēdūxērunt**.
       generātim, adv., *tribe by tribe*, here, *in tribal groups as follows.*
7   **intervāllum, -ī**, n., *interval, distance (apart).*
       paribus intervāllīs: *at . . .* , ablative of attendant circumstances.
       Harūdēs . . . Suēbōs (8): *Harudes, Marcomani, Triboci, Vangiones, Nemetes,
           Sedusii, Suebi* (names of German tribes).
8   **carrus, -ī**, m., *cart.*
9   **circumdō, circumdare, circumdedī, circumdatus**, *to surround, encircle.*
       omnemque aciem suam (8) **. . . circumdedērunt**: forming a semi-circle
           around the backs and sides of each tribe as it lined up for battle.
   ***spēs, -ēī**, f., *hope, expectation, prospect.*
       nē qua spēs . . . relinquerētur: what construction? For the use of **qua**,
           see page 24, note to line 47.
       Eō: = **In raedās et carrōs.**
       mulierēs: subject or object of **imposuērunt**? Use the context to decide.
10 **proficīscentēs . . . flentēs** (11): again, use the context to determine which
       participle modifes which noun or pronoun.
       pandō, pandere, pandī, passus, *to spread out, stretch out, extend.*
11 **fleō, flēre, flēvī, flētus**, *to cry, weep.*
       implōrō, -āre, -āvī, -ātus, *to implore, beg.*
       nē sē . . . trāderent: stating the plea of the **mulierēs**. Who is the subject
           of the verb and what is the antecedent of **sē**? Distinguish between this
           nē clause and the one in line 9.

Caesar's speech had the expected result of rallying the legions. A subsequent meeting between Caesar and Ariovistus ended abruptly when German cavalry tried to provoke Caesar's bodyguard into fighting. Two Roman negotiators sent later in Caesar's place were seized and charged with spying. Battle was imminent. In addition to his main camp Caesar built a smaller camp a short distance beyond the Germans to secure the supply route, providing it with two legions and auxiliaries. For six days Caesar lined up his troops for battle without a definitive engagement. Finally, he learned from prisoners that the Germans would not fight before the new moon on the advice of their women soothsayers. Caesar takes the initiative and compels the Germans to fight.

51. Postrīdiē eius diēī Caesar praesidiō utrīsque castrīs quod satis esse   1
vīsum est relīquit; ālāriōs omnēs in cōnspectū hostium prō castrīs   2
minōribus cōnstituit, quod minus multitūdine mīlitum legiōnāriōrum   3
prō hostium numerō valēbat, ut ad speciem ālāriīs ūterētur; ipse triplicī   4
īnstrūctā aciē usque ad castra hostium accessit. Tum dēmum necessāriō   5
Germānī suās cōpiās castrīs ēdūxērunt generātimque cōnstituērunt   6
paribus intervāllīs, Harūdēs, Marcomanōs, Tribocōs, Vangionēs,   7
Nemetēs, Sedusiōs, Suēbōs, omnemque aciem suam raedīs et carrīs   8
circumdedērunt, nē qua spēs in fugā relinquerētur. Eō mulierēs   9
imposuērunt, quae ad proelium proficīscentēs mīlitēs passīs manibus   10
flentēs implōrābant nē sē in servitūtem Rōmānīs trāderent.   11

Comprehension Questions

1. With what in mind did Caesar post his auxiliaries in front of his smaller camp? (2–4)
2. How were the Romans lined up for battle? How were the Germans? (4–9)
3. To prevent flight and raise the stakes for their warriors, in what unusual way were the German women employed? (9–11)

VOCABULARY REVIEW

accēdō, -ere, accessī, accessūrus,
  to advance, go, come
ēdūcō, -ere, ēdūxī, ēductus, *to*
  lead or *take (out)*
eō, adv., *to that place, there*
impōnō, -ere, imposuī,
  impositus, *to place on, put*
manus, -ūs, f., *hand*
mulier, mulieris, f., *woman; wife*
multitūdō, multitūdinis, f.,
  (large) number or *size*
nē, conj. + subjn., *so that . . . not*

numerus, -ī, m., *number*
postrīdiē, adv., *on the day after*
prō, prep. + abl., *in front of*
raeda, -ae, f., *coach, wagon*
relinquō, -ere, relīquī, relictus, *to*
  leave behind, leave
servitūs, servitūtis, f., *slavery*
trādō, -ere, trādidī, trāditus, *to*
  hand over, deliver, surrender
tum, adv., *then*
uterque, utraque, utrumque, *each*
  (of two)

12 *singulī, -ae, -a, *single, individual.*
   quaestor, quaestōris, m., *quaestor (the finance and supply officer).*
   praeficiō, praeficere, praefēcī, praefectus, *to put X in charge of Y* (dat.).
     et quaestōrem praefēcit: *and he put a quaestor in charge (of one legion).*
        Lieutenants will command five legions and a quaestor the sixth.
13 *utī:* an alternate form of **ut.**
   testis, testis, testium, m., *witness.*
     testēs suae . . . virtūtis: in apposition to **eōs:** *as witnesses of his bravery.*
   *quisque, quaeque, quodque, *each (one).*
   ipse: to whom does this refer? See page 28, note to line 4.
   *cornū, -ūs, n., *horn;* of an army, *wing.*
     ā dextrō cornū: *on the. . . .* The preposition *ab* often means *in* or *on* with
        respect to placement on the military field.
14 **eam partem:** the corresponding or left side of the enemy.
   minimē firmam: *the least strong, the weakest.*
15 **Ita:** modifying **ācriter** and anticipating the result clause in lines 16–17.
   in hostēs . . . impetum fēcērunt: the idiom *impetum facere in* + acc.
     means *to make an attack against, to attack.*
   itaque: = **et ita.**
16 *repente, adv., *suddenly.*
   spatium, -ī, n., *space; opportunity.*
   *pīlum, -ī,** n., *javelin.*
     spatium pīla . . . coniciendī (17): *an opportunity for hurling javelins.* The
        genitive of a gerund may take a neuter object, as in this case with **pīla.**
        Note the meaning of *in,* *against,* here and in line 15 above.
17 **rēiciō, rēicere, rēiēcī, rēiectus,** *to throw back; to throw aside.*
   *comminus, adv., *hand to hand, at close quarters.*
   pugnātum est: *the fighting continued = they fought.* The passive of **pugnāre**
        and of a few other verbs is used impersonally to emphasize action.
18 *cōnsuētūdō, cōnsuētūdinis,** f., *custom, habit.*
   *phalanx, phalangis,** f., *phalanx.*
     celeriter ex cōnsuētūdine suā phalange factā: *quickly entering into their*
        usual formation; lit., *quickly having made a phalanx according to their habit.*
        Each German tribe has closed its ranks, with soldiers in front locking
        shields and those behind holding their shields overhead.
19 **quī:** a relative clause of characteristic: *(of the sort) who (would).*
20 **īnsiliō, īnsilīre, īnsiluī,** *to jump on, leap.*
   *scūtum, -ī,** n., *shield.*
   revellō, revellere, revellī, revulsus, *to tear X* (acc.) *from Y* (abl.).
   dēsuper, adv., *from above.*
   Cum . . . pulsa (21): = **Cum . . . pulsa esset,** *Although. . . .*
23 *premō, premere, pressī, pressus,** *to press hard, bear down on.*
   P. Crassus adulēscēns: *the young Publius Crassus* (son of Marcus Crassus,
        one of the First Triumvirate).
24 *expedītus, -a, -um, *lightly armed; unhampered, free.*
   versor, versārī, versātus sum + **inter** + acc., *to be involved in; to be in.*
25 *subsidium, -ī,** n., *reinforcement; support, help.*
     nostrīs subsidiō: *as . . . for . . . ,* double dative.

Each side gains early advantages in fierce fighting until Publius Crassus arrives with timely reinforcements.

52. Caesar singulīs legiōnibus singulōs lēgātōs et quaestōrem praefēcit, 12
utī eōs testēs suae quisque virtūtis habēret; ipse ā dextrō cornū, quod 13
eam partem minimē firmam hostium esse animadverterat, proelium 14
commīsit. Ita nostrī ācriter in hostēs signō datō impetum fēcērunt itaque 15
hostēs repente celeriterque prōcurrērunt ut spatium pīla in hostēs 16
coniciendī nōn darētur. Rēiectīs pīlīs comminus gladiīs pugnātum est. 17
At Germānī celeriter ex cōnsuētūdine suā phalange factā impetūs 18
gladiōrum excēpērunt. Repertī sunt complūrēs nostrī quī in phalangem 19
īnsilīrent et scūta manibus revellerent et dēsuper vulnerārent. Cum 20
hostium aciēs ā sinistrō cornū pulsa atque in fugam coniecta esset, ā 21
dextrō cornū vehementer multitūdine suōrum nostram aciem 22
premēbant. Id cum animadvertisset P. Crassus adulēscēns, quī equitātuī 23
praeerat, quod expedītior erat quam eī quī inter aciem versābantur, 24
tertiam aciem labōrantibus nostrīs subsidiō mīsit. 25

Comprehension Questions

1. What measure did Caesar take to inspire his men? (12–13)
2. Why did Caesar choose to be on his right wing when the fight began? What might have been his battle plan? (13–15)
3. Fighting against a formidable German phalanx, what dramatic action did some Romans take? (19–20)
4. Notwithstanding a rout of the German left wing, what unexpected development on the other wing nearly cost Caesar a victory? How did Publius Crassus, acting on his own, reclaim the victory? (20–25)

VOCABULARY REVIEW

ācer, ācris, ācre, *fierce*
adulēscēns, adulēscentis, *young*
at, conj., *but*
celer, celeris, celere, *swift, quick*
committō, -ere, commīsī, commissus, *to entrust;* with **proelium,** *to enter battle*
complūrēs, -ēs, -a, *several; many*
coniciō, -ere, coniēcī, coniectus, *to throw, hurl*
dexter, dextra, dextrum, *right*
dō, dare, dedī, datus, *to give*
excipiō, -ere, excēpī, exceptus, *to*

receive
firmus, -a, -um, *firm, strong*
gladius, -ī, m., *sword*
impetus, -ūs, m., *attack*
labōrō, -āre, -āvī, -ātus, *to work; to struggle, be in trouble*
prōcurrō, -ere, prōcurrī, prōcursūrus, *to run* or *rush forward*
pugnō, -āre, -āvī, -ātūrus, *to fight*
sinister, sinistra, sinistrum, *left*
vulnerō, -āre, -āvī, -ātus, *to wound, inflict a wound*

26   *restituō, restituere, restituī, restitūtus, *to restore, revive, renew.*
    terga vertērunt: the expression *tergum vertere, *to turn one's back,* came to mean *to turn and flee, to flee.*
27   *priusquam, conj., *before, until.*
    neque prius . . . quam: place **priusquam,** which is often divided in this manner, after **dēstitērunt** in your translation. The division of a compound word into two parts with one or several words in between is called tmesis.
    dēsistō, dēsistere, dēstitī, dēstitus + inf., *to cease, stop* (doing).
    *passus, -ūs, m., *step, pace.*
        mīlia passuum . . . quīnque (28): accusative of extent of space, expressing the distance traveled from the battle site (**ex eō locō**) to the river. Roman miles were measured in terms of a pace, the distance of one full step or about five feet. A thousand paces, *mīlle passūs,** was a Roman mile, though it was slightly shorter than our mile. The plural is expressed with a partitive genitive: **mīlia passuum,** *miles.*
28   *circiter, adv., *about.*
    *perpaucī, -ae, -a, *very few.*
    vīribus cōnfīsī: *trusting in their strength.* Note the difference in form in the plural between the two similar looking nouns **vīrēs** (abl. pl., **vīribus**), *strength,* and **vir, virī** (abl. pl., **virīs**), *man.*
29   trānō, -āre, -āvī, *to swim across.*
    *contendō, contendere, contendī, contentus, *to attempt, try.*
    *salūs, salūtis, f., *safety, (a means of) survival.*
    In hīs (30): *Among the latter,* an idiomatic meaning of **hic;** compare **ille,** *the former.*
30   nāvicula, -ae, f., *small boat.*
    dēligō, -āre, -āvī, -ātus, *to fasten, tie up.*
    *rīpa, -ae, f., *bank* (of a river), *shore.*
    *nancīscor, nancīscī, nactus sum, *to chance upon, find.*
    eā: ablative of means referring to **nāvicula,** but best translated as *in it.*
31   *eques, equitis, m., *horseman;* pl., *cavalry.*
32   Suēbus, -a, -um, *of the Suebi tribe, Sueban* (of the same tribe that Ariovistus came from).
    **nātiō, nātiōnis, f., *people, race.*
    nātiōne: *by birth,* ablative of respect.
    domō: explain the rule of place to which and place from which that applies to **domus.**
33   ēdūxerat . . . dūxerat: the subject is Ariovistus, but in the second instance **dūxerat** is short for **in mātrimōnium dūxerat,** *he had married.*
    Nōricus, -a, -um, *of Noricum, Norican* (referring to the country of Noricum, situated between the Danube and the Alps).
    Vocc. iō, Voccionis, m., *Voccio* (king of Noricum).
    ā frātre missam (34): modifying **quam.**
34   pereō, perīre, periī, peritūrus, irreg., *to perish, die.*
35   occīsa: supply **est.**

With the reserve line in action, the Romans surge. The Germans are soundly beaten and few escape alive.

53. Ita proelium restitūtum est, atque omnēs hostēs terga vertērunt 26
neque prius fugere dēstitērunt quam ad flūmen Rhēnum mīlia passuum 27
ex eō locō circiter quīnque pervēnērunt. Ibi perpaucī aut vīribus cōnfīsī 28
trānāre contendērunt aut lintribus inventīs sibi salūtem repperērunt. In 29
hīs fuit Ariovistus, quī nāviculam dēligātam ad rīpam nactus eā 30
profūgit; reliquōs omnēs cōnsecūtī equitēs nostrī interfēcērunt. Duae 31
fuērunt Ariovistī uxōrēs, ūna Suēba nātiōne, quam domō sēcum 32
ēdūxerat, altera Nōrica, rēgis Vocciōnis soror, quam in Galliā dūxerat ā 33
frātre missam; utraque in eā fugā periit. Fuērunt duae fīliae: hārum 34
altera occīsa, altera capta est. 35

Caesar, De bello Gallico I.51–53

Comprehension Questions

1. It was generally recognized that the Gauls and Germans mounted a furious charge but then crumbled under a disciplined attack. Where is the truth of that observation borne out in this battle?
2. How were the few German survivors able to cross the Rhine? (28–29)
3. Although Ariovistus escaped, his leadership of the loose confederation of German tribes was effectively eliminated, and he has no more role to play in *De bello Gallico*. What happened to his wives and daughters? (31–35)
4. The Roman historian Tacitus tells us that the Germans were strongly monogamous except among the noble class. Caesar alludes to the advantage for Ariovistus in having a second wife. What was it? (31–34)

VOCABULARY REVIEW

alter, altera, alterum, *the other (of two), the second*
    alter . . . alter, *one . . . the other*
cōnsequor, -ī, cōnsecūtus sum, *to follow after; to overtake*
duo, duae, duo, *two*
fīlia, -ae, f., *daughter*
fugiō, -ere, fūgī, fugitūrus, *to flee, run away*
frāter, frātris, m., *brother*
ibi, adv., *in that place, there*
inveniō, -īre, invēnī, inventus, *to come upon, find*
mīlle, indecl. noun and adj., *a thousand*
    mīlia, mīlium, n. pl., *thousands*
occīdō, -ere, occīdī, occīsus, *to kill*
profugiō, -ere, profūgī, *to flee, escape*
quīnque, *five*
rēx, rēgis, m., *king*
soror, sorōris, f., *sister*
tergum, -ī, n., *back*
uxor, uxōris, f., *woman; wife*
vertō, -ere, vertī, versus, *to turn*
vīs, acc., **vim**, abl., **vī**, f., *force; attack*
    vīrēs, vīrium, f. pl., *strength*

BOOK II: THE CAMPAIGN AGAINST THE BELGAE

In the space of a single summer Caesar had completed two important campaigns. He led his army to winter quarters in the territory of the Sequani slightly earlier than the season required. Leaving Labienus in command, he set off for northern Italy to hold the assizes there.
Caesar, *De bello Gallico*, I.54

The first year of the campaign was an unqualified success. Caesar's troops had distinguished themselves against two formidable opponents and as they entered their second year in Gaul they would be more seasoned and more confident in their commander's leadership and vision. Caesar had taken a bold step in wintering his troops outside the Province; the proximity of occupational forces put the Aedui and Sequani on notice that they were to act as Roman intermediaries in central Gaul. Caesar also ordered a reconnaissance of the Belgae in northern Gaul. Disturbing reports came from there.

> The Belgae, as he explained, occupy a third of the whole land of Gaul. The reasons for their conspiracy were these. First, they were afraid that if all the rest of Gaul were subdued, our army would proceed to invade their country. Second, they were being urged by certain of the other Gauls; some of these did not take any more kindly to having a Roman army wintering in their country and establishing itself there, than they had to the prolonged presence of the Germans, and others were eager for a change of overlords, simply because they were fickle and fond of change. There was also the fact that in Gaul royal power was commonly seized by those powerful individuals who had the means of hiring mercenaries; realization that this would be more difficult to do if the Romans had control of the country prompted yet others to support the conspiracy.
> Caesar, *De bello Gallico*, II.1

By the summer of 57 Caesar had raised two new legions to join the six he already had in Gaul. Marching quickly into the northern interior he first reached the tribe of the Remi, who readily capitulated and provided valuable information to Caesar. He learned that all the northern tribes were contributing to the war effort against him and that banded together they were approaching his legions. Caesar set up camp at the river Aisne and garrisoned Bibrax, a Remi stronghold eight miles away. Topography and a masterful use of Roman auxiliaries gave Caesar the advantage. Failing to take the Romans head-on, the Belgae decided to split up and return to defend their individual homelands. That decision played into Caesar's hand; using the Remi and Aedui as wedges, Caesar forced the two largest tribes, the Bellovaci and Suessiones, into submission without bloodshed, and then moving east he received the surrender of the Ambiani.

> Beyond the boundaries of the Ambiani, lived the Nervii. He made inquiries about them, their character, and customs, and this is what he discovered. Traders were not given access to their country; they did not allow wine and other luxuries to be imported because they considered that things of that kind softened men's spirits and weakened their courage. They were fierce and courageous,

and they bitterly denounced the rest of the Belgae for having thrown away their traditional courage by surrendering to the Romans. They were emphatic that they were not going to send envoys or accept peace on any terms.

When we had marched through their territory for three days, Caesar discovered from prisoners that the river Sambre was only ten miles away from our camp and that on the far side of it all the Nervian forces had taken up position, waiting for us to arrive. The Atrebates and the Viromandui, neighbouring tribes whom they had persuaded to join them in the risks of war, were with them. He was told that they were also waiting for the forces of the Atuatuci, who were already on the way. . . .

On receiving this information, he sent out patrols with some centurions to choose a good site for a camp. A large number of the Belgae who had surrendered and other Gauls were following, marching with us. Some of these, as he later discovered from prisoners, having noted the marching routine of my army during those days, went by night and told the Nervii that between one legion and the next we had a long baggage train, and so when the first legion reached camp, the rest would be a long way behind; it would be quite easy to attack it while the men were still carrying their heavy packs. Once the first legion had been routed and the baggage train plundered, the rest would not dare to make a stand against them.

Caesar, De bello Gallico, II.15–17

Caesar broke camp and approached the Sambre. A suitable camp site had been found on a hill overlooking the river. The site was uphill—an advantage in charging and a disadvantage to an attacking army—and near water; that this apparently secure location would be the site of the fiercest battle of the Gallic War did not enter Caesar's mind.

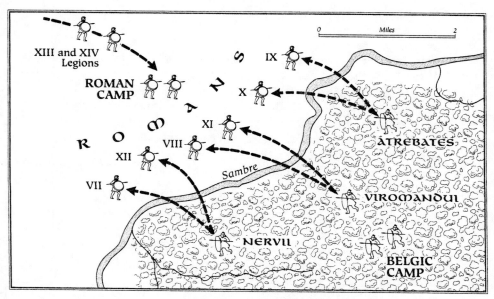

Diagram of the battle of the Sambre River

1   **Locī . . . , quem locum**: the antecedent of a relative pronoun may be repeated in the relative clause and need not be translated a second time.
    haec: *as follows*, looking ahead to lines 2–8.
    castrīs: *for (the purpose of building) a camp*, dative of purpose.
    dēligō, dēligere, dēlēgī, dēlēctus, *to pick out, choose*.
    collis: Caesar surveys two hills; the first is the site where the Roman camp will be built, the second (line 3) is where the Nervii are hiding.

2   **summum, -ī**, n., *highest point, top*.
    aequāliter, adv., *evenly*.
    *****dēclīvis, -is, -e**, *sloping downward*.
    Sabis, Sabis, acc., **Sabim**, m., *the Sambre* (a river in Belgium).

3   **vergō, vergere**, *to slope down, be inclined down to, descend*.
    acclīvitās, acclīvitātis, f., *ascent, upward slope*.
    parī acclīvitāte collis: *a hill with a similar ascent*, ablative of description.

4   *****adversus, -a, -um** + dat., *opposite, facing*.
    contrārius, -a, -um, *facing; across the way*.
    adversus huic et contrārius: *(directly) facing this (hill*, on which the Romans were to build their camp) *and across the way*.
    passūs circiter ducentōs: *for about . . .* , accusative of extent of space.
    īnfimus, -a, -um, *lowest*; here, *at the bottom*.
    *****apertus, -a, -um**, *open, exposed, bare* (of trees).
    ab: *on, along*.

5   *****superior, superior, superius**, gen., **superiōris**, *higher*.
    silvestris, -is, -e, *wooded, covered with trees*.
    intrōrsus, adv., *within*.
    posset: the subject, *it*, refers to the wooded part of the hill, **superior pars**.

6   *****occultus, -a, -um**, *hidden, secret, concealed*.
    in occultō: *in hiding*.
    secundum, prep. + acc., *along, alongside*.

7   **statiō, statiōnis**, f., *lookout post, detachment* (of soldiers or cavalry).
    *****altitūdō, altitūdinis**, f., *height; depth*.

8   **pedum circiter trium**: (of) *about . . . .*

9   **omnibus cōpiīs**: *with . . .* , ablative of accompaniment without **cum**.

10   **ratiō ōrdōque**: treat as a single idea: *general arrangement*.
    *****agmen, agminis**, n., *marching line, army on the march*.
    aliter, adv., *otherwise, differently*.
    aliter sē habēbat ac: (it) *was different from (what). . . .* ; lit., (it) *held itself differently than. . . .*
    *****Nerviī, -ōrum**, m. pl., *the Nervii* (one of the principal tribes of Belgium).
    dēferō, dēferre, dētulī, dēlātus, irreg., *to carry along; to report*.

11   **cōnsuētūdine suā**: *by his custom = as was his custom*.

12   **expedītās**: *in light marching order* (carrying hand tools and weapons only).
    *****impedīmentum, -ī**, n., *impediment, obstacle*; pl., *baggage train*.

13   *****collocō, -āre, -āvī, -ātus**, *to place, position*.
    collocārat: = **collocāverat**.
    proximē: *most recently*
    cōnscrībō, cōnscrībere, cōnscrīpsī, cōnscrīptus, *to enlist; to raise, levy*.

14   **agmen claudere**, idiom, *to close the column = to bring up the rear*.

BOOK II

Caesar describes the location chosen for the Roman camp.

18. Locī nātūra erat haec, quem locum nostrī castrīs dēlēgerant: collis 1
ab summō aequāliter dēclīvis ad flūmen Sabim, quod suprā 2
nōminavimus, vergēbat; ab eō flūmine parī acclīvitāte collis nāscēbātur 3
adversus huic et contrārius, passūs circiter ducentōs īnfimus apertus, ab 4
superiōre parte silvestris, ut nōn facile intrōrsus perspicī posset. Intrā 5
eās silvās hostēs in occultō sēsē continēbant. In apertō locō secundum 6
flūmen paucae statiōnēs equitum vidēbantur. Flūminis erat altitūdō 7
pedum circiter trium. 8
19. Caesar, equitātū praemissō, subsequēbātur omnibus cōpiīs, sed 9
ratiō ōrdōque agminis aliter sē habēbat ac Belgae ad Nerviōs dētulerant. 10
Nam quod hostibus appropinquābat, cōnsuētūdine suā Caesar sex 11
legiōnēs expedītās dūcēbat; post eās tōtīus exercitūs impedīmenta 12
collocārat; inde duae legiōnēs quae proximē cōnscrīptae erant tōtum 13
agmen claudēbant praesidiōque impedīmentīs erant. 14

Comprehension Questions

1. Briefly describe the area. Give an exact description of the second hill. (1–8)
2. In an effort to explain how he was caught in an ambush of near deadly proportions, here and throughout the account Caesar introduces reasons and explanations for his failure to foresee it. How would the landscape of the second hill and the presence of a small enemy detachment have blinded him to the possibility of an ambush? (3–8)
3. The Nervii were expecting a staggered Roman column with baggage trains between each legion. In fact, what was the Roman marching formation? Why did it differ from what the Nervii were expecting? (9–14)

VOCABULARY REVIEW
---

appropinquō, -āre, -āvī + dat., *to approach, draw near (to)*
claudō, -ere, clausī, clausus, *to shut, close*
collis, collis, collium, m., *hill*
contineō, -ēre, continuī, contentus, *to hold, keep*
ducentī, -ae, -a, *two hundred*
facile, adv., *easily*
inde, adv., *then, following that*
intrā, prep. + acc., *inside, within*
nāscor, -ī, nātus sum, *to be born; to*

arise
nātūra, -ae, f., *nature; layout*
nōminō, -āre, -āvī, -ātus, *to name, mention*
pēs, pedis, m., *foot*
post, prep. + acc., *after, behind*
praemittō, -ere, praemīsī, praemissus, *to send ahead*
sex, *six*
subsequor, -ī, subsecūtus sum, *to follow close behind*
suprā, adv., *above, previously*

15   **funditor, funditōris,** m., *slinger.*
      sagittārius, -ī, m., *archer.*

16   **Cum . . . illī . . . , interim legiōne̱s sex** (19): *While they* (i.e., the enemy cavalry) . . . , (meanwhile) *the six legions.* . . .

17   **recipiō, recipere, recēpī, receptus,** *to receive; to take back.*
      *sē recipere, *to retreat, withdraw.*
          sē (16) **. . . in silvās ad suōs reciperent ac rūrsus ex silvā:** the distinction made is that between a scattered retreat into different parts of the forest, **in silvās,** and a unified attack from one spot, **ex silvā.**

18   **neque nostrī . . . audērent** (19): = **et nostrī . . . nōn audērent.**
      longius quam quem ad fīnem: *beyond where;* lit., *farther than to which end* (i.e., the line of the trees).
      porrigō, porrigere, porrēxī, porrēctus, *to reach out, stretch, extend.*
      porrēcta loca aperta: *the stretch of open ground;* lit., *the extended open places.*

19   **pertineō, pertinēre, pertinuī,** *to reach; to end.*
      cēdentēs: = **eōs** (i.e., the enemy cavalry) **cēdentēs.**

20   ***opus, operis,** n., *work; building, fortifying.*
      dīmētior, dīmētīrī, dīmēnsus sum, *to measure out.*
          opere dīmēnsō: *once the work was measured out,* or, more fully, *once the measurements for the fortification were taken.* **Dīmētīrī** is a rare deponent whose perfect participle is passive in meaning.
      *mūniō, -īre, -īvī, -ītus, *to fortify; to construct, build.*

21   **prīma impedīmenta:** *the first (sign of the) baggage train* = *the front of the baggage train.*

22   ***lateō, latēre, latuī,** *to lie hidden, be concealed.*

23   ***conveniō, convenīre, convēnī, conventus,** *to come together; to come to an agreement; to be agreed upon.*
          quod tempus . . . convēnerat: *the (very) time . . . that had been agreed upon.* **Tempus** also governs **committendī proeliī** with the meaning *the time (fixed upon for the purpose) of, the time for.*
      ut: *(exactly) as* . . . , anticipating the maneuver in the next line.

24   **cōnfirmō, -āre, -āvī, -ātus,** *to strengthen; to encourage.*
      atque ipsī sēsē cōnfirmāverant: *and (as) they themselves had encouraged each other (to do).*
      omnibus cōpiīs: ablative of accompaniment without **cum.**
      prōvolō, -āre, -āvī, -ātūrus, *to fly forward; to rush forward.*

25   **Hīs:** supply **equitibus.**
      prōturbō, -āre, -āvī, -ātus, *to drive away in confusion, scatter pell-mell.*
      incrēdibilī: *with (such) amazing.*

26   **et . . . et . . . et** (27): *both . . . and . . . and.* This is a good example of polysyndeton, using more conjunctions than usual to impress the reader here with the sudden appearance of the enemy everywhere at once.

27   **in manibus nostrīs:** *in our midst, among us;* lit., *in our hands.*
      vidērentur: supply **esse.**

28   **adversō colle:** *up the hill;* lit., *by means of the hill facing* (them).
      eōs: also governed by **ad.**

29   ***contendō, contendere, contendī, contentus,** *to rush, hasten, race.*

Skirmishes near the river precede a furious outpouring from the woods that catches the Romans by surprise.

Equitēs nostrī cum funditōribus sagittāriīsque flūmen trānsgressī 15
cum hostium equitātū proelium commīsērunt. Cum sē illī identidem in 16
silvās ad suōs reciperent ac rūrsus ex silvā in nostrōs impetum facerent, 17
neque nostrī longius quam quem ad fīnem porrēcta loca aperta 18
pertinēbant cēdentēs īnsequī audērent, interim legiōnēs sex, quae 19
prīmae vēnerant, opere dīmēnsō castra mūnīre coepērunt. 20
Ubi prīma impedīmenta nostrī exercitūs ab eīs quī in silvīs abditī 21
latēbant vīsa sunt, quod tempus inter eōs committendī proeliī 22
convēnerat, ut intrā silvās aciem ōrdinēsque cōnstituerant atque ipsī 23
sēsē cōnfirmāverant, subitō omnibus cōpiīs prōvolāvērunt impetumque 24
in nostrōs equitēs fēcērunt. Hīs facile pulsīs ac prōturbātīs, incrēdibilī 25
celeritāte ad flūmen dēcucurrērunt ut paene ūnō tempore et ad silvās et 26
in flūmine et iam in manibus nostrīs hostēs vidērentur. Eādem autem 27
celeritāte adversō colle ad nostra castra atque eōs quī in opere occupātī 28
erant contendērunt. 29

Comprehension Questions

1. Caesar gives an aerial, cinematic view of all the players and all the action at once. In lines 15–20, what two operations were happening simultaneously?
2. What visual cue were the Nervii awaiting before their attack? (21–22) According to their information, why would this have been the best time to strike?
3. By letting us watch the ambush unfold from the enemy point of view, what enemy strengths does Caesar wish us to see as we look into the woods? How does he create suspense through word order? (21–25)
4. Cite words in lines 25–29 that convey the ease and rapidity of the ambush.

VOCABULARY REVIEW

audeō, -ēre, ausus sum, *to dare*
cēdō, -ere, cessī, cessūrus, *to go;*
   to retreat, withdraw
celeritās, celeritātis, f., *speed*
coepī, coepisse, coeptus,
   defective verb, *I began*
dēcurrō, -ere, dē(cu)currī,
   dēcursus, *to run down*
identidem, adv., *repeatedly*
īnsequor, -ī, īnsecūtus sum, *to*
   follow after, pursue
interim, adv., *meanwhile*

occupātus, -a, -um, *engaged*
paene, adv., *almost*
prīmus, -a, -um, *first*
rūrsus, adv., *again*
trānsgredior, -ī, trānsgressus
   sum, *to cross*
ūnō tempore, *at one time,*
   simultaneously
veniō, -īre, vēnī, ventūrus, *to*
   come
videor, -ērī, vīsus sum, *to be seen;*
   to seem, appear

30 **omnia . . . erant agenda**: *all things had to be done,* a passive periphrastic with
a past tense form of **sum**. In lines 32–34 supply **erat** or **erant** to complete
the passive periphrastics. What case is **Caesarī** and why?
 vexillum, -ī, n., *flag, banner.*
 prōpōnō, prōpōnere, prōposuī, prōpositus, *to put up, raise.*
  vexillum prōpōnendum: the commanding general had a large white
   banner with red lettering that when suspended called men to arms.
31 **īnsigne, īnsignis, īnsignium,** n., *mark, signal, cue, sign.*
 concurrī: an intransitive verb used impersonally in the passive; with
  oportēret translate **concurrī**: *that there be a rush, that the soldiers hurry.*
 tuba, -ae, f., *trumpet.*
  signum tubā dandum (32): the first trumpet blast required a falling into
   ranks, the second (34) gave the order to charge into battle.
32 **ab . . . mīlitēs; quī . . . arcessendī** (33): referring to two different groups of
  soldiers, one (**mīlitēs**) at work on the camp, the other (**quī**) farther afield
  in search of materials to build the embankment around the camp, *(Some)*
  soldiers . . . , (while others,) who . . . , had to be sent for.
 paulō longius: *a little farther;* lit., *farther by a little.*
 *****agger, aggeris,** m., *mound; rampart;* here, *material for the embankment* (i.e.,
  wood, stones, and turf that formed the defensive wall of a camp).
33 **aciēs īnstruenda; mīlitēs cohortandī; signum dandum** (34): the final but
  hurried actions prior to an engagement, where between assuming battle
  formation and giving the signal to advance, the general typically gave
  each legion words of encouragement.
 *****cohortor, cohortārī, cohortātus sum,** *to exhort, encourage.*
34 **Quārum rērum**: *But . . . of these things.* A form of **quī** placed at the start of
  one sentence and referring to someone or something in the previous
  sentence as its antecedent is called a linking **quī**. Use a personal or
  demonstrative pronoun in place of the relative in your translation.
35 **incursus, -ūs,** m., *assault, attack.*
 difficultātibus . . . subsidiō (36): what construction? See page 24, line 56.
36 **scientia atque ūsus mīlitum, quod . . . poterant,** (38) **et**
  quod . . . Caesar . . . vetuerat (40): *(first) the (military) knowledge and*
  experience of his soldiers, because . . . they were able . . . , and (second) the fact
  that Caesar had told (them) not to. . . .
 superiōribus proeliīs: *in earlier battles.*
37 **quid fierī oportēret**: indirect question, object of **praescrībere** (38).
 nōn minus commodē . . . quam: litotes, *no less easily . . . than = just as easily*
  . . . as; take after **praescrībere** in your translation.
38 **praescrībō, praescrībere, praescrīpsī, praescrīptus,** *to describe beforehand;*
  to decide, determine.
39 **nisi mūnītīs castrīs**: *until the camp had been fortified;* lit., *unless with the camp*
  fortified.
40 **propinquitās, propinquitātis,** f., *nearness, proximity.*
 nihil iam: *not any longer, no longer,* stronger than **nōn iam.**
 imperium, -ī, n., *command, order.*
41 **quae vidēbantur**: *what seemed (best).*
42 **administrō, -āre, -āvī, -ātus,** *to manage, carry out, handle.*

*As Caesar rapidly organizes his troops for a response, he knows that he can rely
on his officers to respond well independently of him.*

20. Caesarī omnia ūnō tempore erant agenda: vēxillum prōpōnendum 30
quod erat īnsigne cum ad arma concurrī oportēret; signum tubā 31
dandum; ab opere revocandī mīlitēs; quī paulō longius aggeris petendī 32
causā prōcesserant arcessendī; aciēs īnstruenda; mīlitēs cohortandī; 33
signum dandum. Quārum rērum magnam partem temporis brevitās et 34
incursus hostium impediēbat. Hīs difficultātibus duae rēs erant 35
subsidiō, scientia atque ūsus mīlitum, quod, superiōribus proeliīs 36
exercitātī, quid fierī oportēret, nōn minus commodē ipsī sibi 37
praescrībere quam ab aliīs docērī poterant, et quod ab opere singulīsque 38
legiōnibus singulōs lēgātōs Caesar discēdere nisi mūnītīs castrīs 39
vetuerat. Hī propter propinquitātem et celeritātem hostium nihil iam 40
Caesaris imperium exspectābant sed per sē quae vidēbantur 41
administrābant. 42

Comprehension Questions

1. Over what operations did Caesar personally take charge? (30–34)
2. How do the verb forms and asyndeton add to the sense of urgency? (30–34)
3. What two obstacles prevented Caesar from successfully accomplishing these operations? (34–35)
4. What two factors were in Caesar's favor? (35–40)
5. Words and phrases related to time and speed thread their way through the account as pointed reminders of the sizable advantage the Nervii had and the extreme difficulty Caesar faced in containing the surprise attack and reversing it. Find examples that illustrate this in lines 22–84.

VOCABULARY REVIEW

agō, -ere, ēgī, āctus, *to drive; to do done; to happen*

arcessō, -ere, arcessīvī, arcessītus, *to summon, send for*

brevitās, brevitātis, f., *shortness*

concurrō, -ere, concurrī, concursūrus, *to rush, hurry*

difficultās, difficultātis, f., *difficulty, trouble*

doceō, -ēre, docuī, doctus, *to teach, instruct, show*

exerceō, -ēre, -uī, -itus, *to train*

exspectō, -āre, -āvī, -ātus, *to wait for, expect*

fīō, fierī, factus sum, irreg., *to be*

impediō, -īre, -īvī, -ītus, *to hinder, hamper, prevent*

nisi, conj., *unless, if . . . not*

oportet, -ēre, oportuit, impersonal, *it is necessary*

paulum, -ī, n., *a little*

prōcēdō, -ere, prōcessī, prōcessūrus, *to go forward, go off*

revocō, -āre, -āvī, -ātus, *to recall*

scientia, -ae, f., *knowledge*

vetō, -āre, vetuī, vetitus, *to forbid, tell X not to*

44 ***fors, fortis**, f., *luck, chance.*
  *offerō, offerre, obtulī, oblātus, irreg., *to offer, present.*
  quam (43) in partem fors obtulit: *wherever chance took him;* lit., *to which side chance presented.*
  Mīlitēs . . . sustinērent (47): lines 44–47 summarize Caesar's brief exhortation to the 10th legion prior to giving them the signal to fight.
45 **ōrātiō, ōrātiōnis**, f., *speech.*
  nōn longiōre ōrātiōne . . . quam utī: *with (= in) a speech no longer than (this), that. . . . ,* followed by an indirect command.
  prīstinus, -a, -um, *original; former, earlier.*
46 **neu**, conj., *nor, and . . . not.*
  animō: *in . . . ,* ablative of specification.
47 **nōn longius:** take with **aberant.** What degree of the adverb is **longius?** Note that the adverbial forms of **longus** build on the meaning *far.*
  *tēlum, -ī, n., *weapon* (for hurling).
  quam quō tēlum: *than (the distance) to which a weapon.*
48 ***adigō, adigere, adēgī, adāctus**, *to drive; to throw, hurl.*
49 ***item**, adv., *likewise, in the same way*
  pugnantibus: for the participle supply a noun that fits the context.
50 ***exiguitās, exiguitātis**, f., *shortness; shortage.*
  dīmicō, -āre, -āvī, -ātūrus, *to fight.*
  ad dīmicandum: *to . . . ;* note the gerund of purpose here and the gerundives of purpose with **ad** in lines 51–52.
51 **nōn modo . . . sed etiam**, conj., *not only . . . but also.*
  īnsigne, īnsignis, n., *mark, badge, decoration.*
  The **īnsignia** were worn by soldiers to indicate their position in a particular legion and cohort. The most obvious **īnsignia** were the crests on the helmets, which varied in shape and color and were removed from the helmet and stored while marching.
  accomodō, -āre, -āvī, -ātus, *to put on, attach.*
  galea, -ae, f., *helmet.*
52 **scūtīs:** *from . . . ,* dative of separation, usually governed by a verb compounded with **ab, dē,** or **ex** and meaning *to take away.*
  tegimentum, -ī, n., *covering, wrapping.*
  tegimenta: leather coverings protected the metal shields when not in use.
  dēfuerit: contrary to the normal sequence of tenses that would have called for an imperfect subjunctive here, the perfect subjunctive stresses the reality of the outcome, that there really was no time to do what needed to be done. In this way Latin distinguishes a real from a potential result.
54 ***cōnsistō, cōnsistere, cōnstitī**, *to stop; to take up a position.*
  Quam quisque ab (52) opere in partem . . . quaeque . . . signa . . . ad haec cōnstitit: take **cōnstitit** with both clauses: *Each (soldier coming) from the fortifying (of the camp) stopped wherever . . . and which(ever) standards . . . at these he took up a position.* For **quam in partem,** *wherever,* compare lines 43–44 above.
  in quaerendīs suīs: supply **signīs.**
  dīmittō, dīmittere, dīmīsī, dīmissus, *to send away; to let slip away, lose.*

Caesar exhorts the 10th legion and then finds the 9th in disarray.

21. Caesar, necessāriīs rēbus imperātīs, ad cohortandōs mīlitēs quam in 43
partem fors obtulit dēcucurrit et ad legiōnem decimam dēvēnit. Mīlitēs 44
nōn longiōre ōrātiōne cohortātus quam utī suae prīstinae virtūtis 45
memoriam retinērent neu perturbārentur animō hostiumque impetum 46
fortiter sustinērent, quod nōn longius hostēs aberant quam quō tēlum 47
adigī posset, proeliī committendī signum dedit. Atque in alteram 48
partem item cohortandī causā profectus pugnantibus occurrit. Temporis 49
tanta fuit exiguitās hostiumque tam parātus ad dīmicandum animus ut 50
nōn modo ad īnsignia accommodanda sed etiam ad galeās induendās 51
scūtīsque tegimenta dētrahenda tempus dēfuerit. Quam quisque ab 52
opere in partem cāsū dēvēnit quaeque prīma signa cōnspexit ad haec 53
cōnstitit nē in quaerendīs suīs pugnandī tempus dīmitteret. 54

Comprehension Questions

1. What explanation does Caesar give for arriving first at the 10th legion? (43–44)
2. What three commands did Caesar give in his short exhortation to the 10th legion? (45–47)
3. Why was he forced to cut short his speech? (47–48)
4. What two reasons does Caesar give for the general confusion and disarray among the soldiers of his 9th legion? (49–52)
5. What three essential operations were the soldiers of the the 9th legion unable to complete? What danger would each failure invite?
6. What unusual step did each soldier of the 9th legion take at this point? Why was it crucial for the soldiers to do so? (52–54)

VOCABULARY REVIEW

cōnspiciō, -ere, cōnspexī, cōnspectus, *to catch sight of, see*
dētrahō, -ere, dētrāxī, detractus, *to draw off, take away, remove*
dēveniō, -īre, dēvēnī, dēventūrus, *to come*
imperō, -āre, -āvī, -ātus, *to order*
induō, -ere, induī, indūtus, *to put on*
longus, -a, -um, *long*

occurrō, -ere, occurrī, occursūrus + dat., *to meet, come upon*
parātus, -a, -um, *prepared, ready*
retineō, -ēre, retinuī, retentus, *to retain, keep*
sustineō, -ēre, sustinuī, sustentus, *to hold up; to withstand*

55   **Caesar . . . possent** (69): a single sentence, revealing first through Caesar's eyes the terrible situation, then his energetic response. Use the participles and primary verbs as anchors for several independent sentences.
    cohortātiō, cohortātiōnis, f., *exhortation, address.*
      ab . . . cohortātiōne: *from (= after) his address of (= to).* . . .
56   *****urgeō, urgēre, ursī,** *to press hard.*
    duodecimae legiōnis (57): an inexperienced legion, recruited in 58 B.C.
57   *****cōnfertus, -a, -um,** *crowded together, closely packed.*
58   **quārtae cohortis:** genitive with **centuriōnibus, signiferō,** and **signō** (59).
    signifer, signiferī, m., *standard bearer*
59   *****āmittō, āmittere, āmīsī, āmissus,** *to send away; to let go; to lose.*
60   **prīmipīlus, -ī,** m., *first centurion* (the leading centurion in a legion, commanding the first cohort).
    P. Sextius Baculus, -ī, m., *Publius Sextius Baculus.*
61   *****cōnficiō, cōnficere, cōnfēcī, cōnfectus,** *to complete; to exhaust, overcome.*
62   **tardus, -a, -um,** *slow, lagging, hanging back.*
    reliquōs esse tardiōrēs . . . vīdit (64): renewing the indirect statement: (*and Caesar also) saw that the rest were hanging back even more.*
    *****novissimī, -ōrum,** m. pl., *the newly recruited; rearguard.*
    ab novissimīs: in lines 62–64 **ab** should be translated as *in* or *on.*
    dēserō, dēserere, dēseruī, dēsertus, *to leave, abandon, desert.*
63   *****īnferior, īnferior, īnferius,** gen., **īnferiōris,** *lower.*
    ex īnferiōre locō: i.e., from the river bank up to the Roman camp.
    hostēs (63) **neque . . . subeuntēs intermittere . . . neque ūllum esse** (65): (*but) neither did the enemy stop coming up . . . nor was there any.* . . .
    *****subeō, subīre, subiī, subitūrus,** irreg., *to come up (to), approach.*
64   **intermittō, intermittere, intermīsī, intermissus,** *to leave off, cease, stop.*
    latus, lateris, n., *side ; flank* (of an army).
    *****īnstō, īnstāre, īnstitī, īnstatūrus,** *to press forward.*
    augustum, -ī, n., *confined space; critical moment, crisis.*
65   *****summittō, summittere, summīsī, summissus,** *to send as help.*
66   **mīlitī:** dative of separation, see page 42, note to line 52.
67   **nōminātim,** adv., *by name.*
68   **signa īnferre:** = **signa ferre.**
    manipulus, -ī, m., *maniple* (a unit consisting of 120 men).
    laxō, -āre, -āvī, -ātus, *to widen, spread out.*
    *****quō,** conj. + subjn., *in order that, so that* (introducing a purpose clause that contains a comparative).
69   **Cuius adventū:** *And at his arrival* or *And by his arrival.* For the linking **quī,** see page 40, note to line 34.
    *****redintegrō, -āre, -āvī, -ātus,** *to renew, revive.*
70   **prō sē quisque:** *each soldier to the best of his ability* (lit., *for himself).*
    extrēmus, -a, -um, *extreme; extremely dangerous.*
    extrēmīs suīs: *personally perilous, life threatening.*
71   **opera, -ae,** f., *work, task.*
    nāvō, -āre, -āvī, -ātus, *to devote oneself to.*
    operam nāvāre, *to join in fully, go all out.*
    tardō, -āre, -āvī, -ātus, *to slow down, hinder, check.*

In paragraphs 22–24, the 9th and 10th legions on the left have forced the Atrebates back across the river, while the 11th and 8th legions in the center have pushed the Viro-mandui down to the river (consult the diagram on page 35). That, however, has exposed the camp on two sides. As Caesar arrives, he sees that the Nervii, pressing the 12th and 7th legions on the right, are on the verge of outflanking the Romans and seizing the camp. The Roman cavalry, auxiliaries, and camp servants have already scattered.

25. Caesar ab decimae legiōnis cohortātiōne ad dextrum cornū 55
profectus, ubi suōs urgērī signīsque in ūnum locum collātīs duodecimae 56
legiōnis cōnfertōs mīlitēs sibi ipsōs ad pugnam esse impedīmentō vīdit, 57
quārtae cohortis omnibus centuriōnibus occīsīs signiferōque interfectō, 58
signō āmissō, reliquārum cohortium omnibus ferē centuriōnibus aut 59
vulnerātīs aut occīsīs, in hīs prīmipīlō P. Sextiō Baculō, fortissimō virō, 60
multīs gravibusque vulneribus cōnfectō ut iam sē sustinēre nōn posset, 61
reliquōs esse tardiōrēs et nōnnūllōs ab novissimīs dēsertō proeliō 62
excēdere ac tēla vītāre, hostēs neque ā fronte ex īnferiōre locō subeuntēs 63
intermittere et ab utrōque latere īnstāre et rem esse in angustō vīdit, 64
neque ūllum esse subsidium quod summittī posset, scūtō ab novissimīs 65
ūnī mīlitī dētractō, quod ipse eō sine scūtō vēnerat, in prīmam aciem 66
prōcessit centuriōnibusque nōminātim appellātīs reliquōs cohortātus 67
mīlitēs signa īnferre et manipulōs laxāre iussit, quō facilius gladiīs ūtī 68
possent. Cuius adventū spē illātā mīlitibus ac redintegrātō animō, cum 69
prō sē quisque in cōnspectū imperātōris etiam in extrēmīs suīs rēbus 70
operam nāvāre cuperet, paulum hostium impetus tardātus est. 71

Comprehension Questions

1. Why was the 12th legion fighting ineffectually? (55–57)
2. What effect do the ablatives absolute create? What is their climax? (58–61)
3. How did the soldiers react to the massive loss of centurions? (62–63)
4. What unusual step did Caesar take? What was the result? (65–71)

VOCABULARY REVIEW

adventus, -ūs, m., *arrival*
cohors, cohortis, cohortium, f., *cohort*
cōnferō, cōnferre, contulī, collātus, irreg., *to bring together, gather*
cupiō, -ere, cupīvī, cupītus, *to desire, wish, want*
duodecimus, -a, -um, *twelfth*

excēdō, -ere, excessī, excessus, *to go out; to depart, withdraw*
frōns, frontis, frontium, f., *front*
gravis, -is, -e, *heavy; serious*
novus, -a, -um, *new*
paulum, adv., *a little, somewhat*
ūllus, -a, -um, *any*
vir, virī, m., *man*
vulnus, vulneris, n., *wound*

72   **iūxtā**, adv., *nearby.*

73   **monuit ut**: translate in the sense of *he instructed them to let X* (nom.) *do Y* (subjunctive).

74   **coniungō, coniungere, coniūnxī, coniūnctus,** *to join together, connect.*
      ***convertō, convertere, convertī, conversus,** *to turn, wheel around.*
        et conversa signa in . . . īnferrent: *and, upon wheeling around, to advance against* (lit., *and bear turned standards against*). . . . Caesar by pulling his 7th and 12th legions together and placing them back-to-back (an inference from the phrase **conversa signa**) intends to create an oblong formation that will offer protection in the back of the line and enable his men to fight on all sides.
        Quō factō: *After this was done.*
        cum aliīs aliī: *since they . . . to each other.* See page 16, note to line 10 for a similar usage.

75   **timērent nē . . . circumvenīrentur (76)**: how is **nē** translated after verbs of fearing? See page 18, note to line 22.
      āversus, -a, -um, *turned away, with one's back turned.*
      āversī: i.e., with their backs to the enemy.
      ***circumveniō, circumvenīre, circumvēnī, circumventus,** *to surround.*

76   **audācius . . . fortius**: what degree are these adverbs?

77   **legiōnum duārum**: the 13th and 14th legions.
      novissimus, -a, -um, *most recent; last in position.*
        ***novissimum agmen**: *the rear line, the rear.* Compare the meaning of **novissimī** on page 44, note to line 62.

78   **praesidiō impedīmentīs fuerant**: what construction? See page 24, line 56.
      cursus, -ūs, m., *running; speed; step.*
        cursū incitātō: *with quickened step, at full speed.*
      in summō colle (79): the ridge of this hill was located behind the Roman camp, and it had a view of the fighting below.

79   ***T. Labiēnus, -ī,** m., *Titus Labienus.*
      Titus Labienus was Caesar's most trusted and able lieutenant, who in the Civil War crossed over to Pompey's side. Presently, in command of the 9th and 10th legions, he has pursued the Atrebates into the woods.

80   **potior, potīrī, potītus sum** + abl., *to take possession of, capture.*
      quae rēs . . . gererentur: indirect question introduced by **cōnspicātus (81)**. In a military setting, the idiom ***rem gerere,** *to conduct business = to fight a battle.*

81   ***cōnspicor, cōnspicārī, cōnspicātus sum,** *to catch sight of, notice, see.*
      Quī cum: *And when they* (i.e., the 10th legion).

82   ***cālō, cālōnis,** m., *camp servant.*
      ex equitum et cālōnum fugā: take with **cognōvissent (83)**.
      quō in locō rēs esset: the interrogative adjective **quō**, modifying **locō**, has been pulled out of the prepositional phrase for emphasis; similarly, **quantōque in perīculō** later in the line. What subjunctive clause is used here?

83   **nihil ad celeritātem sibi reliquī fēcērunt**: *they hurried* (to the site of the battle) *as quickly as they could;* lit., *they made nothing of a remainder for themselves* (= *they left nothing undone*) *in respect to speed.*

Caesar regroups the 12th and 7th legions. Help arrives.

26. Caesar, cum septimam legiōnem, quae iūxtā cōnstiterat, item urgērī   72
ab hoste vīdisset, tribūnōs mīlitum monuit ut paulātim sēsē legiōnēs   73
coniungerent et conversa signa in hostēs īnferrent. Quō factō cum aliīs   74
aliī subsidium ferrent neque timērent nē āversī ab hoste circum-   75
venīrentur, audācius resistere ac fortius pugnāre coepērunt.   76
   Interim mīlitēs legiōnum duārum quae in novissimō agmine   77
praesidiō impedīmentīs fuerant, proeliō nūntiātō, cursū incitātō in   78
summō colle ab hostibus cōnspiciēbantur, et T. Labiēnus castrīs hostium   79
potītus et ex locō superiōre quae rēs in nostrīs castrīs gererentur   80
cōnspicātus decimam legiōnem subsidiō nostrīs mīsit. Quī cum ex   81
equitum et cālōnum fugā, quō in locō rēs esset quantōque in perīculō et   82
castra et legiōnēs et imperātor versārētur, cognōvissent, nihil ad   83
celeritātem sibi reliquī fēcērunt.   84

Comprehension Questions

1. Seeing that the 7th legion was in similar trouble, Caesar has ordered the two legions to assemble into a defensive posture called an **orbis** or *circle*. More accurately described as a hollow square, the **orbis** was a four-sided formation that had evened corners and was several men deep on all sides. Describe the positive results. (74–76)
2. Caesar says of the 13th and 14th legions, **ab hostibus cōnspiciēbantur** (79). From Caesar's perspective, what purpose did his two rearguard legions serve in turning the fight in favor of the Romans?
3. Across the river, what important success has Titus Labienus had with his two legions? From his higher position, what did Labienus see that prompted him to send back the 10th legion? (79–80)
4. What in particular did the 10th legion surmise from the scattering of cavalry and camp servants that caused concern?

VOCABULARY REVIEW

aliī . . . aliī, *some . . . others*
audāx, audācis, *bold*
incitō, -āre, -āvī, -ātus, *to spur on, drive forward*
moneō, -ēre, -uī, -itus, *to advise; to*

instruct
resistō, -ere, restitī, *to resist*
septimus, -a, -um, *seventh*
summus, -a, -um, *highest; greatest; the top of*

85 Hōrum adventū: i.e., of the tenth legion.
    commūtātiō, commūtātiōnis, f., *change, reversal, turnaround.*
    est facta: = facta est.
    ut: introducing three separate result clauses with the subjects nostrī,
        cālōnēs, and equitēs at the head of each one. Note the asyndeton.
86 prōcumbō, prōcumbere, prōcubuī, prōcubitūrus, *to fall down, collapse.*
    nostrī (85) etiam quī . . . prōcubuissent: *even those of our men who.* . . . ,
        a relative clause of characteristic.
    innītor, innītī, innīxus sum + abl., *to lean (on), support oneself (with).*
87 inermis, -is, -e, *without weapons, unarmed.*
    inermēs: modifying cālōnēs and placed here to contrast with armātīs
        (supply hostibus) in the next line.
88 occurrō, occurrere, occurrī, occursūrus + dat., *to rush against, attack.*
    turpitūdō, turpitūdinis, f., *shame, disgrace.*
    turpitūdinem fugae: the Roman cavalry was doubly disgraced; it had
        been quickly routed by the enemy at the river and, after regrouping at
        the camp, it scattered again at the approach of the Nervii.
89 praeferō, praeferre, praetulī, praelātus, irreg., *to carry in front.*
    se praeferre + dat., *to surpass, outperform, outfight.*
90 *extrēmus, -a, -um, *last, final.*
91 *praestō, praestāre, praestitī, praestātus, *to excel; to exhibit, display.*
    iacentibus: translate substantively: *those lying = the fallen.* Take the dative
        with īnsisterent (92) not proximī.
92 īnsistō, īnsistere, īnstitī + dat., *to stand on.*
    *dēiciō, dēicere, dēiēcī, dēiectus, *to throw down; to kill.*
93 coacervō, -āre, -āvī, -ātus, *to pile up.*
    supersum, superesse, superfuī, irreg., *to be left, remain, survive.*
    hīs (92) dēiectīs et . . . , quī superessent, ut . . . , . . . conicerent (94): *but
        even after these men* (referring to proximī, 91) *had been killed and* . . . ,
        (those) who survived, as (if) . . . , *began to hurl.* . . .
    tumulus, -ī, m., *mound, hill.*
94 intercipiō, intercipere, intercēpī, interceptus, *to catch in flight; to retrieve,*
        pick up.
    nēquīquam, adv., *in vain, without cause.*
    nōn nēquīquam: modifying iūdicārī dēbēret.
    tantae virtūtis hominēs iūdicārī dēbēret ausōs esse: *it should be judged
        (that these were) men of great courage (who) dared to.* . . .
96 *inīquus, -a, -um, *uneven; unfavorable.*
    quae: *(actions) that* . . . , referring to the infinitives in the previous lines and
        object of redēgerat (97).
    facilia: predicate adjective, modifying quae.
97 redigō, redigere, redēgī, redāctus, *to drive back; to render, make.*

Wounded Romans reenter the fray as surviving Nervii fight on boldly.

27. Hōrum adventū tanta rērum commūtātiō est facta, ut nostrī etiam 85
quī vulneribus cōnfectī prōcubuissent scūtīs innīxī proelium 86
redintegrārent, cālōnēs perterritōs hostēs cōnspicātī etiam inermēs 87
armātīs occurrerent, equitēs vērō, ut turpitūdinem fugae virtūte 88
dēlērent, omnibus in locīs pugnae sē legiōnāriīs mīlitibus praeferrent. 89
At hostēs etiam in extrēmā spē salūtis tantam virtūtem 90
praestitērunt, ut, cum prīmī eōrum cecidissent, proximī iacentibus 91
īnsisterent atque ex eōrum corporibus pugnārent; hīs dēiectīs et 92
coacervātīs cadāveribus, quī superessent, ut ex tumulō, tēla in nostrōs 93
conicerent et pīla intercepta remitterent: ut nōn nēquīquam tantae 94
virtūtis hominēs iūdicārī dēbēret ausōs esse trānsīre lātissimum flūmen, 95
ascendere altissimās rīpās, subīre inīquissimum locum; quae facilia ex 96
difficillimīs animī magnitūdō redēgerat. 97

Caesar, De bello Gallico II.18–27

Comprehension Questions

1. What effect did the arrival of the 10th legion have on the wounded, the camp servants, and the cavalry? As each group reenters the battle, what small detail does Caesar add that raises the level of their bravery? (85–89)
2. The grim determination of the enemy is highlighted in lines 90–94. How do the words for falling, lying, dying, and fighting reflect this determination?
3. Lines 94–97 seem to commend the enemy's courage in attempting the impossible. But looked at differently, how could the list of infinitives and superlatives be taken as Caesar's self-defense against possible charges of inadequate preparation for such an ambush? In your answer, comment on Caesar's use of topography here and at the start of this episode. (94–97)

VOCABULARY REVIEW

altus, -a, -um, *tall, high, steep*
ascendō, -ere, ascendī, ascēnsus, *to climb*
cadāver, cadāveris, n., *dead body*
cadō, -ere, cecidī, cāsus, *to fall; to die, be killed*
dēbeō, -ēre, dēbuī, dēbitus, *to owe; (one) ought, should, must*
dēleō, -ēre, dēlēvī, dēlētus, *to*
destroy; to remove
difficilis, -is, -e, *difficult*
facilis, -is, -e, *easy*
iaceō, -ēre, iacuī, iacitūrus, *to lie*
lātus, -a, -um, *broad, wide*
perterreō, -ēre, -uī, -itus, *to terrify, greatly alarm*
remittō, -ere, remīsī, remissus, *to send back; to throw back*

1   *crēber, crēbra, crēbrum, *repeated, numerous, frequent.*
      excursiō, excursiōnis, f., *a running out; sortie, sally, small raid.*
2   faciēbant: the Atuatuci are the subjects.
      *vāllum, -ī, n., *wall; rampart* (a wall of earth topped with stakes).
        vāllō . . . castellīs (3): ablative of means with circummūnītī (4).
3   circuitus, -ūs, m., *circumference.*
        pedum duodecim . . . quīndecim mīlium: the height and circumference
          respectively of the rampart; in circuitū applies only to the second
          measurement, but pedum applies to both.
      *castellum, -ī, n., dim. of castra, *fortified settlement; lookout tower.*
4   circummūniō, -īre, -īvī, -ītus, *to surround with walls; to hem in.*
      oppidō: = in oppidō.
      vīnea, -ae, f., *vineyard;* military, *movable shed* (for cover during a siege).
      exstruō, exstruere, exstrūxī, exstrūctus, *to build up, construct.*
        vīneīs āctīs aggere exstrūctō: sheds were brought up (vīneās agere) to
          the enemy walls to help construct a ramp (agger) for the siege.
5   *turris, turris, turrium, acc., turrim, f., *tower* (rolled up a ramp in a siege).
      cōnstituī: passive infinitive or perfect indicative? What are the clues?
6   increpitō, increpitāre, *to blame; to taunt.*
      irrīdēre (5) . . . increpitāre: historical infinitives; translate as imperfects.
      *māchinātiō, māchinātiōnis, f., *machine, mechanical device.*
        quod . . . īnstruerētur: *because, (they said), (it) was being built.* . . .
      spatium, -ī, n., *space; distance.*
      ā tantō spatiō: *at such a distance, so far away.*
7   *quīnam, quaenam, quodnam, emphatic interrogative adjective, *what.*
      quibusnam manibus: *but really, with what hands.*
      praesertim, adv., *especially, particularly.*
      tantulus, -a, -um, diminutive of tantus, *such a small, such a short.*
8   statūra, -ae, f., *stature, body size, height.*
        praesertim (7) hominēs tantulae statūrae: in apposition to the subject of
          the main verb, cōnfīderent (10): *did they, (being) particularly men of.* . . .
      hominibus Gallīs . . . contemptuī est: *(it) is an object of . . . for the.* . . . ,
        double dative.
      prae, prep. + abl., *before; in comparison with.*
9   contemptus, -ūs, m., *contempt, scorn.*
11   movērī et appropinquāre: supply turrim as the subject of the infinitives.
      moenia, moenium, n. pl., *walls* (often the defensive walls of a town).
12   inūsitātus, -a, -um, *unusual, unfamiliar, extraordinary.*
      ad hunc modum: *in the following manner, as follows;* lit., *to this manner.*
        quī ad hunc modum locūtī . . . dīxērunt (16): join the verbs together:
          who addressing (Caesar) as follows said (that). . . .
13   ops, opis, f., *power; help, aid.*
14   quī . . . possent (15): *since they could . . . ,* a causal quī clause.
15   sē suaque omnia: objects of permittere. *Sua means *their possessions.*
      potestās, potestātis, f., *power, control, authority.*
      permittō, permittere, permīsī, permissus, *to give over, surrender.*

*Fifty years earlier 6,000 Cimbri and Teutones had been left in northern Gaul to guard the
cattle and possessions of the Germans during their drive south. After the defeat of the
Germans to Marius, the Atuatuci, as they were called, settled in fortified towns or
oppida. Recently, the Atuatuci had set out to help the Nervii, but hearing of the failed
ambush they returned home and holed themselves up in one **oppidum** that was "ringed
around by very high, sheer rocks except at one point, where there was a gently sloping
approach no more than 200 feet wide."*

30. Ac prīmō adventū exercitūs nostrī crēbrās ex oppidō excursiōnēs   1
faciēbant parvulīsque proeliīs cum nostrīs contendēbant; posteā vāllō   2
pedum duodecim in circuitū quīndecim mīlium crēbrīsque castellīs   3
circummūnītī oppidō sēsē continēbant. Ubi vīneīs āctīs aggere exstrūctō   4
turrim procul cōnstituī vīdērunt, prīmum irrīdēre ex mūrō atque   5
increpitāre vōcibus, quod tanta māchinātiō ā tantō spatiō īnstruerētur;   6
quibusnam manibus aut quibus vīribus praesertim hominēs tantulae   7
statūrae (nam plērumque hominibus Gallīs prae magnitūdine corporum   8
suōrum brevitās nostra contemptuī est) tantī oneris turrim in mūrō sēsē   9
collocāre posse cōnfīderent?   10
31. Ubi vērō movērī et appropinquāre moenibus vīdērunt, novā atque   11
inūsitātā speciē commōtī lēgātōs ad Caesarem dē pāce mīsērunt, quī ad   12
hunc modum locūtī: Nōn sē exīstimāre Rōmānōs sine ope dīvīnā   13
bellum gerere, quī tantae altitūdinis māchinātiōnēs tantā celeritāte   14
prōmovēre possent; sē suaque omnia eōrum potestātī permittere   15
dīxērunt.   16

Comprehension Questions

1. Describe the circumvallation (the ring of ramparts and towers). (2–4)
2. In using the historical infinitives **irrīdēre** (5) and **increpitāre** (6), Caesar
   wants his audience to hear the Atuatuci laughing and taunting the Romans.
   What has struck them as humorous about the siege preparations of the
   Romans? What costly miscalculation have they made about sieges? (9–10)
3. Explain the reason for their swift change in attitude. (11–16)

VOCABULARY REVIEW
---

dīvīnus, -a, -um, *divine, of the gods*
duodecim, *twelve*
Gallus, -a, -um, *Gallic*
irrīdeō, -ēre, irrīsī, irrīsus, *to
    laugh at, mock, ridicule*
loquor, -ī, locūtus sum, *to speak*
modus, -ī, m., *measure; manner*
mūrus, -ī, m., *wall*

onus, oneris, n., *burden, weight*
oppidum, -ī, n., *town, stronghold*
parvulus, -a, -um, *very small*
pāx, pācis, f., *peace*
procul, adv., *far away, at a distance*
**prōmoveō, -ēre, prōmōvī,
    prōmōtus**, *to push forward*
quīndecim, *fifteen*

17 **dēprecor, dēprecārī, dēprecātus sum,** *to pray for, beg, strongly request.*
    Ūnum petere ac dēprecārī: *(They added that) they sought and were requesting one thing only. . . .* , anticipating their request in line 19, **nē . . . dēspoliāret.**
    prō: *in accordance with, in keeping with.*
    clēmentia, -ae, f., *kindness, forgiveness, mercifulness.*
18 **mānsuētūdō, mānsuētūdinis,** f., *gentleness, compassion.*
    quam: *(examples of) which.*
    *statuō, statuere, statuī, statūtus, to set up; to determine, decide.
      sī . . . statuisset . . . , nē (19): *if . . . he (Caesar) should have decided that . . . , (the envoys asked) that he not. . . .*
    Atuatucī, -ōrum, m. pl., *the Atuatuci.*
19 **sē. . . . Sibi:** referring to the Atuatuci; **sibi** is dative with **inimīcōs (20).**
    dēspoliō, -āre, -āvī, -ātus, *to rob; to deprive X* (acc.) *of Y* (abl.).
    *fīnitimī, -ōrum, m. pl., *neighbors,* here, *neighboring tribes.*
20 **invideō, invidēre, invīdī, invīsus** + dat., *to envy, resent, be jealous of.*
    ā quibus: *and against them;* lit., *from whom.*
21 **praestat, praestāre** + dat., *it is preferable, it is better.*
    Sibi praestāre: *It would be better for them* = *They preferred.*
    *cāsus, -ūs, m., *a falling down; misfortune, calamity, disaster.*
    in eum cāsum: i.e., the inability to defend themselves against attack.
    dēdūcō, dēdūcere, dēdūxī, dēductus, *to bring away; to force.*
    quīvīs, quaevīs, quidvīs, *any at all, any.*
22 **quam:** *than,* drawing the comparison between **patī** and **interficī.**
    cruciātus, -ūs, m., *torture.*
23 **dominor, dominārī, dominātus sum,** *to dominate, rule.*
    *cōnsuēscō, cōnsuēscere, cōnsuēvī, cōnsuētus, to be accustomed.
24 **magis cōnsuētūdine suā quam meritō eōrum:** *in keeping with his usual treatment (of the enemy) more than through a deserving act of theirs.*
25 **ariēs, arietis,** m., *ram;* military, *battering-ram.*
26 **attingō, attingere, attigī, attāctus,** *to touch.*
    *dēdo, dēdere, dēdidī, dēditus, to give up, surrender.
    *dēditiō, dēditiōnis, f., surrender.
    esse: *(that) there would be;* lit., *(that) there was.*
27 **in Nerviīs:** *in the case of the Nervii, in his settlement with the Nervii.*
28 **quam . . . iniūriam:** *any harm.* For **quam,** see page 24, note to line 47.
    dēditīcius, -a, -um, *having surrendered.*
    dēditīciīs populī Rōmānī: *on those who have surrendered (and are subjects) of the Roman people.*
29 **quae . . . dīxērunt:** the fuller version of the terse surrender might read: **sē omnia quae ā Caesare imperārentur facere dīxērunt.**
31 **prope:** adverbial, take with **adaequārent (32).**
    summam . . . altitūdinem: *the full height.*
    acervus, -ī, m., *heap, pile, stack.*
32 **adaequō, -āre, -āvī, -ātus,** *to make equal in height; to reach* (the level of).
    et tamen circiter parte tertiā: *but with, however, nearly a third part.*
33 **patefaciō, patefacere, patefēcī, patefactus,** *to throw open, open.*
    ūtor, ūtī, ūsus sum + abl., *to use; to enjoy; to take advantage of.*

The Atuatuci will surrender but with one urgent request.

Ūnum petere ac dēprecārī: sī forte prō suā clēmentiā ac 17
mānsuētūdine, quam ipsī ab aliīs audīrent, statuisset Atuatucōs esse 18
cōnservandōs, nē sē armīs dēspoliāret. Sibi omnēs ferē fīnitimōs esse 19
inimīcōs ac suae virtūtī invidēre; ā quibus sē dēfendere trāditīs armīs 20
nōn possent. Sibi praestāre, sī in eum cāsum dēdūcerentur, quamvīs 21
fortūnam ā populō Rōmānō patī quam ab hīs per cruciātum interficī, 22
inter quōs dominārī cōnsuēssent. 23
32. Ad haec Caesar respondit: Sē magis cōnsuētūdine suā quam 24
meritō eōrum cīvitātem cōnservātūrum, sī, priusquam mūrum ariēs 25
attigisset, sē dēdidissent: sed dēditiōnis nūllam esse condiciōnem nisi 26
armīs trāditīs. Sē id quod in Nerviīs fēcisset factūrum fīnitimīsque 27
imperātūrum nē quam dēditīciīs populī Rōmānī iniūriam īnferrent. Rē 28
nūntiātā ad suōs, quae imperārentur facere dīxērunt. Armōrum magnā 29
multitūdine dē mūrō in fossam quae erat ante oppidum iactā, sīc ut 30
prope summam mūrī aggerisque altitūdinem acervī armōrum 31
adaequārent, et tamen circiter parte tertiā, ut posteā perspectum est, 32
cēlātā atque in oppidō retentā, portīs patefactīs eō diē pāce sunt ūsī. 33

Comprehension Questions

1. How did the Atuatuci first try to warm up Caesar to their request? (17–19)
2. What was their request and the reason behind it? (19–23)
3. Under what conditions will Caesar treat the Atuatuci leniently? (24–29)
4. Of the different arrangements for treating a subjugated tribe—to put it under the protection of a stronger tribe, to promise it Roman protection, or to annihilate it, usually by deportation into slavery—which one has Caesar offered the Atuatuci? (27–28)

VOCABULARY REVIEW

ante, prep. + acc., *in front of*
audiō, -īre, -īvī, -ītus, *to hear*
cēlō, -āre, -āvī, -ātus, *to hide*
cōnservō, -āre, -āvī, -ātus, *to save, preserve*
dēfendō, -ere, dēfendī, dēfēnsus, *to defend, protect*
forte, adv., *by chance*
fossa, -ae, f., *ditch, trench*
iaciō, -ere, iēcī, iactus, *to throw*
inimīcus, -a, -um + dat.,
unfriendly (to), hostile (to)
meritum, -ī, n., *good deed*
nūllus, -a, -um, *no, none*
patior, patī, passus sum, *to experience; to endure, suffer*
porta, -ae, f., *gate*
prope, adv., *near, nearly*
respondeō, -ēre, respondī, respōnsūrus, *to respond, reply*
sīc, adv., *thus, so, to such a degree*

34 **Sub vesperum:** *Toward evening.*
35 **nē quam ... iniūriam:** compare with page 52, note to line 28.
    oppidānī, -ōrum, m. pl., *townspeople.*
    Illī: i.e., the Atuatuci, the grammatical subject of **fēcērunt** (42).
    ante: adverbial, with **initō ... cōnsiliō** (36).
36 **ineō, inīre, iniī, initus,** irreg., *to enter upon;* of a plan, *to form.*
37 *****dēdūcō, dēdūcere, dēdūxī, dēductus,** *to withdraw, remove.*
        nostrōs praesidia (36) **dēductūrōs ... servātūrōs:** indirect statement
            with **crēdiderant.** Take **praesidia,** here referring to the guards
            stationed in the defense towers, as object of both infinitives.
    dēnique, adv., *at least.*
    partim ... partim (38): *some ... others,* in apposition to **illī** (35).
38 **cum eīs ... armīs:** translate as a unit; **cum** also governs **scūtīs.**
    cortex, corticis, m., *bark.*
39 **vīmen, vīminis,** n., *branch, (pliant) stick* or *twig.*
    intexō, intexere, intexuī, intextus, *to weave in, interweave.*
    quae: neuter accusative plural, with **scūtīs** (38) as antecedent.
    subitō: *without planning, on the spur of the moment.*
40 **postulō, -āre, -āvī, -ātus,** *to ask, demand, require.*
    pellis, pellis, pellium, f., *hide, animal skin.*
    indūcō, indūcere, indūxī, inductus, *to bring in;* *to put on, cover, wrap.*
    quā: *where;* lit., *by which (way).*
    arduus, -a, -um, *steep.*
41 *****mūnītiō, mūnītiōnis,** f., *a fortifying; fortification, rampart.*
42 *****ēruptiō, ēruptiōnis,** f., *a breaking out, bursting forth, charge.*
        ēruptiōnem facere, *to burst forth, charge (out).*
43 **significātiō, significātiōnis,** f., *signal.*
    ignibus: *by torches,* a common method of communication between posts.
    concursum est, pugnātumque ... est (44): see page 30, note to line 17.
44 **ita ācriter ... ut ā virīs fortibus ... pugnārī dēbuit** (46): *as fiercely as brave*
        men ought to have fought; lit., *as fiercely as by brave men ... fighting ought to*
        have been done.
45 **inīquō locō:** *on ... ,* ablative of place where.
46 **ūnā:** *alone.*
    *****cōnsistō, cōnsistere, cōnstitī** + **in** + abl., *to depend on.*
47 **ad:** adverbial, *about.*
    rēiciō, rēicere, rēiecī, rēiectus, *to throw back; to drive back.*
48 **refringō, refringere, refrēgī, refrāctus,** *to break open.*
49 **sectiō, sectiōnis,** f., *auction* or *sale of captured goods.*
    *****ūniversus, -a, -um,** *all, whole, entire.*
        sectiōnem eius oppidī ūniversam: *the goods of this town in one lot.*
            Buyers accompanying Caesar have purchased in one block all the
                property and townspeople (to be sold later as slaves).
50 **Ab eīs quī ēmerant ... ad eum:** i.e., the buyers and Caesar, respectively.
    capitum: an example of synecdoche, where the part, the heads, stands for
        the whole, the people.
    referō, referre, retulī, relātus, irreg., *to bring back; to report.*
    relātus est mīlium (51): *(it) was reported (to be) of ... = was reported as.*

The Atuatuci prepare and execute a surprise raid from the town.

33. Sub vesperum Caesar portās claudī mīlitēsque ex oppidō exīre 34
iussit, nē quam noctū oppidānī ā mīlitibus iniūriam acciperent. Illī ante 35
initō, ut intellēctum est, cōnsiliō, quod dēditiōne factā nostrōs praesidia 36
dēductūrōs aut dēnique indīligentius servātūrōs crēdiderant, partim 37
cum eīs quae retinuerant et cēlāverant armīs, partim scūtīs ex cortice 38
factīs aut vīminibus intextīs, quae subitō, ut temporis exiguitās 39
postulābat, pellibus indūxerant, tertiā vigiliā, quā minimē arduus ad 40
nostrās mūnītiōnēs ascēnsus vidēbātur, omnibus cōpiīs repente ex 41
oppidō ēruptiōnem fēcērunt. Celeriter, ut ante Caesar imperāverat, 42
ignibus significātiōne factā ex proximīs castellīs eō concursum est, 43
pugnātumque ab hostibus ita ācriter est ut ā virīs fortibus in extrēmā spē 44
salūtis inīquō locō contrā eōs quī ex vāllō turribusque tēla iacerent 45
pugnārī dēbuit, cum in ūnā virtūte omnis spēs salutis cōnsisteret. 46
Occīsīs ad hominum mīlibus quattuor reliquī in oppidum rēiectī sunt. 47
Postrīdiē eius diēī refrāctīs portīs, cum iam dēfenderet nēmō, atque 48
intrōmissīs mīlitibus nostrīs sectiōnem eius oppidī ūniversam Caesar 49
vēndidit. Ab eīs quī ēmerant capitum numerus ad eum relātus est 50
mīlium quīnquāgintā trium. 51

Caesar, *De bello Gallico* II.30–33

Comprehension Questions

1. Why did Caesar remove the Roman garrison from the town? Why is it necessary for him to mention this? (34–35)
2. Why did the Atuatuci expect the Roman guard to miss the raid? (36–37)
3. Describe the shields that some of the Atuatuci were forced to use. (38–40)
4. What clue does Caesar give that he had expected a surprise raid? (42)
5. How does Caesar express admiration for the enemy's valiant effort? (44–46)
6. How many Atuatuci died? How many were sold into slavery? (47–51)

VOCABULARY REVIEW

ante, adv., *earlier, in advance*
ascēnsus, -ūs, m., *climb, approach*
caput, capitis, n., *head*
crēdō, -ere, crēdidī, crēditus, *to
  trust, believe*
emō, -ere, ēmī, ēmptus, *to buy*
ignis, ignis, ignium, m., *fire; torch*
indīligenter, adv., *carelessly*
intrōmitto, -ere, intrōmīsī,

intrōmissus, *to send in*
noctū, adv., *at night*
quīnquāgintā, *fifty*
servō, -āre, -āvī, -ātus, *to save,
  keep, maintain*
vēndō, -ere, vēndidī, vēnditus, *to
  sell*
vesper, m., *evening*

BOOK III: REVOLT IN THE NORTHWEST KINGDOM

Caesar had sent Publius Crassus with one legion to deal with the tribes on the Atlantic seaboard—the Veneti, Venelli, Osismi, Curiosolites, Esubii, Aulerci, and Redones. At about this same time he received information from Crassus that all these tribes had been brought into submission to Rome.

With these operations, peace had been brought to the whole of Gaul. . . . When Caesar's dispatches were read in Rome, a public thanksgiving was decreed lasting 15 days; no one had been granted this honor before.

Caesar, De bello Gallico, II.34–35

Caesar's optimistic assessment would be short-lived. The tribes of the Atlantic seaboard were not to be suppressed so easily. Caesar's winter visit to Illyricum was cut short by alarming news from Crassus that Roman envoys sent to requisition grain from three coastal tribes had been detained on condition that the Romans return their hostages. The ringleaders of the new coalition of anti-Roman tribes were the Veneti:

> Now of all the peoples of the coastal part of that area, the Veneti are by far the strongest. They have a great many ships and regularly sail to and from Britain. When it comes to knowledge and experience of navigation, they leave all the other tribes standing. The sea on that coast is extremely violent and open, and the harbors few and far between. Since the Veneti control these, they are able to exact tolls from almost all who regularly use those waters.
>
> Caesar, De bello Gallico, III.8

Understandably, the Veneti had the most to lose if Rome were to interfere in their affairs. Preparation for war began immediately: Caesar ordered that warships be constructed on the Loire River and a native crew of sailors be assembled to pilot the ships; the Veneti and their allies stockpiled their **oppida**, recruited more men from Britain, and stationed all their ships off the coast of Venetia.

Caesar was well aware that a disturbance in one corner of Gaul could ripple throughout the rest of Gaul, threatening his hard-earned and tenuously held **pāx Gallica**. He knew too that his clearest course of action, and one with potential dividends, was to isolate the revolt in the west. Therefore, he sent Sabinus with three legions to the northern seaboard, Crassus with twelve cohorts to Aquitania, and Labienus with cavalry to the Rhine area in order to cut off support for the revolt and reestablish a Roman presence among wavering tribes. He also hoped to gain a foothold on the north coast where there were valuable harbors and in the southwest where resistance to Rome on the fringes of the Province had been fierce. Caesar took charge of the land expedition against the Veneti, and Brutus, waiting inland until the completion of the ships, was to command the fleet.

> The **oppida** of the Veneti were mostly on the far ends of spits, or headlands. They were sited in such a way that they could not be approached on foot when the tide rushed in from the open sea, as happens regularly every twelve hours; they were not accessible by sea either, because ships would be damaged on the

56

shoals when the tide went down. So in both respects there were problems in attacking such **oppida**.

Sometimes, however, we had the Veneti beaten by the sheer scale of our siegeworks; we managed to keep the sea out with great dams, which we built as high as the walls of their **oppida**. But whenever this happened and the Veneti began to realize the hopelessness of their position, they would bring up numbers of ships, of which they had an unlimited supply, load them with their possessions and retreat to other **oppida** nearby, where they would once more defend themselves by the same advantages of terrain....

The Gauls' own ships were built and rigged in a different way from ours. Their keels were somewhat flatter, so they could cope more easily with the shoals and shallow water when the tide was ebbing; their prows were unusually high, and so were their sterns, designed to stand up to great waves and violent storms.... They used sails made of hides or soft leather, either because flax was scarce and they did not know how to use it, or, more probably, because they thought that with cloth sails they would not be able to withstand the force of the violent Atlantic gales, or steer such heavy ships.

When we encountered these vessels, our only advantage lay in the speed and power of our oars; in other respects the enemy's ships were better adapted for the violent storms and other conditions along that coast. They were so solidly built that our ships could not damage them with rams, and their height made it hard to use missiles against them or seize them with grappling irons. Not only that; when a gale blew up and they ran before it, they could weather the storm more easily and heave to more safely in shallow water, and if left aground by the tide, they had nothing to fear from rocks and reefs. To our ships, on the other hand, all these situations were a source of terror. Caesar, *De bello Gallico*, III.12–13

The outcome of the war with the Veneti would be determined by the first recorded naval battle on the Atlantic Ocean and, if first impressions were to be trusted, it would be a sad mismatch.

Roman warship of the first century B.C.

1   *expugnō, -āre, –āvī, -ātus, *to take by storm, capture.*

2   reprimō, reprimere, repressī, repressus, *to restrain, check, stop.*
     neque . . . reprimī neque eīs nocērī posse (3): the infinitives reprimī
       and nocērī depend on posse: *(and that) neither could . . . be stopped nor*
       could harm be done to them. Nocērī is used impersonally.

3   *classis, classis, classium, f., *fleet.*
     statuit exspectandam classem: supply words as needed: statuit (sibi)
       exspectandam (esse) classem.
     Quae ubi convēnit ac prīmum. . . . (4): *As soon as it arrived and. . . .* ; lit.,
       And when it arrived and first. . . .

5   omnī genere armōrum: in this context, arma refers to both the fighting
     power on board and to the rigging and other equipment of a ship.

6   nostrīs adversae cōnstitērunt: (they) *lined up opposite our ships.*
     *Brūtus, -ī, m., *Decimus Brutus* (a respected officer and commander of the
     fleet, later one of the conspirators in the assassination of Caesar).
       Brūtō . . . vel tribūnīs . . . centuriōnibusque (7): datives with
         cōnstābat (8).

8   attribuō, attribuere, attribuī, attribūtus, *to assign.*
     cōnstō, cōnstāre, cōnstitī, cōnstātūrus, *to take a stand; to be apparent.*
     cōnstat, impersonal, *it is apparent, it is clear.*
     quid agerent: *what they were to do,* the first of two indirect questions that in
       direct speech would be deliberative subjunctives.

9   īnsistō, īnsistere, īnstitī, *to stand on; to follow, pursue.*
     rōstrum, -ī, n., *beak* (of an animal or a ship).
     Rōstrō: *By (ramming them with) a beak.*
     nocērī nōn posse: supply nāvibus hostium and see note to line 2.
     cognōverant: *they knew, they realized.* Cognōscere often has this meaning in
       the perfect.

10   excitō, -āre, -āvī, -ātus, *to construct, build, raise up.*
     turribus autem (9) excitātīs: a concession, *but even if. . . .* Such towers, or,
       more properly, turrets, were installed on ships to give protection and
       the advantage of height to soldiers hurling weapons with catapults.
       See the illustration on page 57 for an example.
     hās: supply turrīs (acc. pl.).
     puppis, puppis, puppium, f., *stern* (the rear of a ship).
     ex: *of, belonging to.*
     superābat: (it) *rose above.*

11   neque . . . possent et: = et . . . nōn possent et.
     ex īnferiōre locō: referring to the main decks and towers of the Roman
     ships, which were lower than the sterns of the ships of the Veneti.
     missa: *(weapons) thrown.*

12   gravius: *more heavily, with a greater impact.*
     accidō, accidere, accidī, *to fall, land.*

BOOK III

Seeing that further attempts to take the Veneti by standard land sieges would be futile, Caesar awaits the arrival of Brutus and the fleet. The Roman naval commanders are in a quandary over how to attack the superior Venetian navy.

14. Complūribus expugnātīs oppidīs Caesar, ubi intellēxit frūstrā 1
tantum labōrem sūmī neque hostium fugam captīs oppidīs reprimī 2
neque eīs nocērī posse, statuit exspectandam classem. Quae ubi convēnit 3
ac prīmum ab hostibus vīsa est, circiter ducentae et vīgintī nāvēs eōrum 4
parātissimae atque omnī genere armōrum ōrnātissimae profectae ex 5
portū nostrīs adversae cōnstitērunt; neque satis Brūtō, quī classī 6
praeerat, vel tribūnīs mīlitum centuriōnibusque, quibus singulae nāvēs 7
erant attribūtae, cōnstābat quid agerent aut quam ratiōnem pugnae 8
īnsisterent. Rōstrō enim nocērī nōn posse cognōverant; turribus autem 9
excitātīs tamen hās altitūdō puppium ex barbarīs nāvibus superābat, ut 10
neque ex īnferiōre locō satis commodē tēla adigī possent et missa ā 11
Gallīs gravius acciderent. 12

Comprehension Questions

1. Referring to pages 56–57, explain why Caesar was making no progress in defeating the Veneti in spite of successful land sieges. (1–3)
2. In the still moment before the beginning of the battle, Caesar lets us see the impressive Venetian squadron through Roman eyes. How many Venetian ships were there and how were they equipped? (4–5)
3. We agonize with the Roman land commanders (Brutus and the commanders on board were not trained naval officers) over what strategy to adopt in facing a navy that seemed impervious to standard naval assaults. Describe the two methods of assault mentioned and why they were unsatisfactory in the present situation. (9–12)

VOCABULARY REVIEW

frūstrā, adv., *in vain*
genus, generis, n., *kind, sort*
labor, labōris, m., *work; effort*
nāvis, nāvis, nāvium, f., *ship*
noceō, -ēre, nocuī, nocitūrus +
  dat., *to harm, do harm (to)*
ōrnātus, -a, -um, *decorated;*

equipped, fitted out
portus, -ūs, m., *harbor, port*
sūmō, -ere, sūmpsī, sūmptus, *to*
  take up; to expend, use up
vel, conj., *or*
vīgintī, *twenty*

13   **erat magnō ūsuī**: (it) *was very useful*; lit., (it) *was for a great use.*
    *falx, falcis, falcium, f., *sickle; sickle-shaped hook.*
    praeacūtus, -a, -um, *sharpened at the end, sharpened.*
14   **īnserō, īnserere, īnseruī, īnsertus**, *to insert, attach.*
    affīgō, affīgere, affīxī, affīxus, *to fasten, lash, strap.*
    *longurius, -ī, m., *long pole.*
        longuriīs: dative with **īnsertae** and **affīxae**: *onto (the ends of) long poles.*
        absimilis, -is, -e, *dissimilar, unlike.*
        nōn absimilī fōrmā mūrālium falcium: *shaped like wall hooks*; lit., *with a
        shape not unlike (the shape) of wall hooks,* comparing the new weapon to a
        familar item in siege warfare, the **falx mūrālis** or *wall hook,* that was
        attached to a long pole and used to pull down stones from the walls of
        besieged cities.
    Hīs: what noun is understood?
15   **cum**: *whenever.* A past tense indicative after **cum** usually denotes repeated
    action, as here, where the sequence of repeated action is established by
    the use of a pluperfect (**comprehēnsī adductīque erant**, 15–16), then an
    imperfect (**praerumpēbantur**, 16).
    fūnis, fūnis, fūnium, m., *rope*; nautical, *halyard* (the rope that raised and
    lowered the sail).
    *antemna, -ae, f., *yardarm* (the wooden spar set at right angles to the mast,
    from which the sail hung).
    mālus, -ī, m. *mast* (the center pole of a ship).
    dēstinō, -āre, -āvī, -ātus, *to fix, fasten, secure.*
    *comprehendō, comprehendere, comprehendī, comprehēnsus, *to catch
    hold of, catch, hook.*
16   **addūcō, addūcere, addūxī, adductus**, *to bring* or *draw to; to draw tight.*
    nāvigium, -ī, n., *boat, ship.*
    rēmus, -ī, m., *oar.*
        nāvigiō rēmīs incitātō: describing the final stage of the elaborate
        maneuver as each Roman ship accelerated to produce the snapping
        action. **Rēmīs** is ablative of means.
    praerumpō, praerumpere, praerūpī, praeruptus, *to break off in front, snap.*
    Quibus: what is the antecedent? How do you translate a linking **quī**?
17   **abscīdō, abscīdere, abscīdī, abscīsus**, *to cut off.*
    Gallicīs nāvibus (18): dative of reference.
18   **vēlum, -ī**, n., *sail.*
    armāmenta, -ōrum, n. pl., *equipment, rigging.*
    ūsus: *control.*
19   **certāmen, certāminis**, n., *contest, battle.*
    positum in: (that) *hinged on. . . .* ; lit., (that was) *placed in.*
20   **eō magis**: *all the more*; lit., *the more by this much.*
21   **paulō fortius** (22): *a little braver (than usual).*
22   ***factum, -ī**, n., *deed.*
23   **propinquus, -a, -um**, *close, nearby, ready.*
    dēspectus, -ūs, m., *view;* + **in** + acc., *view over.*

An equalizer is found as the battle suddenly becomes a test of courage.

Ūna erat magnō ūsuī rēs praeparāta ā nostrīs, falcēs praeacūtae 13
īnsertae affīxaeque longuriīs, nōn absimilī fōrmā mūrālium falcium. Hīs 14
cum fūnēs, quī antemnās ad mālōs dēstinābant, comprehēnsī 15
adductīque erant, nāvigiō rēmīs incitātō praerumpēbantur. Quibus 16
abscīsīs antemnae necessāriō concidēbant, ut, cum omnis Gallicīs 17
nāvibus spēs in vēlīs armāmentīsque cōnsisteret, hīs ēreptīs omnis ūsus 18
nāvium ūnō tempore ēriperētur. Reliquum erat certāmen positum in 19
virtūte, quā nostrī mīlitēs facile superābant, atque eō magis quod in 20
cōnspectū Caesaris atque omnis exercitūs rēs gerēbātur, ut nūllum paulō 21
fortius factum latēre posset; omnēs enim collēs ac loca superiōra, unde 22
erat propinquus dēspectus in mare, ab exercitū tenēbantur. 23

Comprehension Questions

1. The word **praeparāta** (13) reveals that the Romans had developed a secret weapon in advance. What was it and how did it work? (13–16)
2. What one fault in the design of Venetian ships made the successful use of this secret weapon so deadly? (16–19)

VOCABULARY REVIEW

concidō, -ere, concidī, *to fall down*
ēripiō, -ere, ēripuī, ēreptus, *to take away, remove*
fōrma, -ae, f., *form, shape*
Gallicus, -a, -um, *of Gaul, Gallic*
mare, maris, marium, n., *sea*

mūrālis, -is, -e, *of a wall*
pōnō, -ere, posuī, positus, *to place*
praeparātus, -a, -um, *prepared in advance*
unde, adv., *from where*

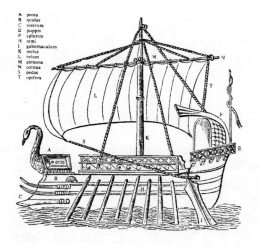

A prora
B oculus
C rostrum
E puppis
F aplustre
H remi
I gubernaculum
K malus
L velum
M antenna
N cornua
S pedes
T opifera

24   **singulās**: *each ship of theirs.*
         bīnī, -ae, -a, *groups of two, two.*
         ternī, -ae, -a, *groups of three, three.*
           bīnae ac ternae nāvēs: *(Roman) ships in groups of two and three.*

25   **circumstō, circumstāre, circumstetī,** *to stand around; to surround.*
           cum (24) . . . circumsteterant: see note to line 15 for **cum** + indicative.
         trānscendō, trānscendere, trānscendī, trānscēnsus + **in** + acc., *to board.*

26   **Quod**: accusative subject of the indirect statement, summarizing the
         developments of the previous sentence. What is unusual about its
         placement and how is the relative best translated?

27   **eī reī**: *for this situation, for the predicament (that they were in).*

29   **ferēbat**: *(it) was blowing.*
         malacia, -ae, f., *calm, dead calm.*
         tranquillitās, tranquillitātis, f., *calm, stillness.*

30   *****exsistō, exsistere, exstitī,** *to surface, arise, come to pass.*
         negōtium, -ī, n., *work; present undertaking, task at hand.*

31   *****opportūnus, -a, -um,** *favorable, well-placed, well-timed.*
         singulās: for translation, see the note to line 24 above.
         cōnsector, cōnsectārī, cōnsectātus sum, *to follow closely, pursue.*

32   **interventus, -ūs,** m., *intervention; coming.*

33   **pervēnerint**: for the mood and tense, see page 42, note to line 52.
         cum: *although.*
         occāsus, -ūs, m., *falling down, setting.*

35   **Venetī, -ōrum,** m. pl., *the Veneti.*
         ōra maritima, -ae, f., *sea-coast.*

36   **cum . . . tum (37)**: *not only . . . but also.*
         iuventūs, iuventūtis, f., *youth, young men.*
         aetās, aetātis, f., *period of one's life, age.*
           graviōris aetātis: *of an older age, of a more advanced age.*

37   **aliquid cōnsilī**: *some wisdom;* lit., *something of (good) counsel.* **Aliquid**
         extends to **dignitātis** in the same way.
         dignitās, dignitātis, f., *worth; rank, influence.*
         nāvium quod (38): *(all) of the ships that,* object of **coēgerant (38).**

38   **ubīque,** adv., *everywhere, anywhere.*

39   **quem ad modum**: *how;* lit., *to what measure.*
           reliquī (38) neque quō sē reciperent neque quem ad modum . . .
             defenderent habēbant (40): *the rest (= survivors) did not have (a place) to*
             where they could . . . nor a way by which (lit., *how*) *they could. . . . :*
             deliberative questions here stated indirectly.

40   **sē suaque omnia**: for the capitulation, compare page 51, line 15.
         In quōs: with **vindicandum (41).**
         eō gravius (41): *all the more severely;* lit., *more severely by this much.*

41   **vindicō, -āre, -āvī, -ātus,** *to claim;* + **in** + acc., *to inflict punishment upon.*
           Caesar vindicandum statuit: for help, see page 58, note to line 3.
         in reliquum tempus: *henceforth, from now on.*

42   **iūs, iūris,** n., *right, customary law, sanctity.*

43   **sub corōnā**: *at an auction, into slavery;* lit., *under the wreath (from placing*
         wreaths on captives to identify them at slave auctions).

Some Venetian ships are boarded, the rest turn to flee.

15. Dēiectīs, ut dīximus, antemnīs, cum singulās bīnae ac ternae nāvēs 24
circumsteterant, mīlitēs summā vī trānscendere in hostium nāvēs 25
contendēbant. Quod postquam barbarī fierī animadvertērunt, 26
expugnātīs complūribus nāvibus, cum eī reī nūllum reperīrētur 27
auxilium, fugā salūtem petere contendērunt. Ac iam conversīs in eam 28
partem nāvibus quō ventus ferēbat, tanta subitō malacia ac tranquillitās 29
exstitit ut sē ex locō movēre nōn possent. Quae quidem rēs ad negōtium 30
cōnficiendum maximē fuit opportūna: nam singulās nostrī cōnsectātī 31
expugnāvērunt ut perpaucae ex omnī numerō noctis interventū ad 32
terram pervēnerint, cum ab hōrā ferē quārtā ūsque ad sōlis occāsum 33
pugnārētur. 34
16. Quō proeliō bellum Venetōrum tōtīusque ōrae maritimae 35
cōnfectum est. Nam cum omnis iuventūs, omnēs etiam graviōris aetātis 36
in quibus aliquid cōnsilī aut dignitātis fuit, eō convēnerant, tum nāvium 37
quod ubīque fuerat in ūnum locum coēgerant; quibus āmissīs reliquī 38
neque quō sē reciperent neque quem ad modum oppida dēfenderent 39
habēbant. Itaque sē suaque omnia Caesarī dēdidērunt. In quōs eō 40
gravius Caesar vindicandum statuit quō dīligentius in reliquum tempus 41
ā barbarīs iūs lēgātōrum cōnservārētur. Itaque omnī senātū necātō 42
reliquōs sub corōnā vēndidit. 43

Caesar, *De bello Gallico* III.14–16

Comprehension Questions

1. **Expugnātīs complūribus nāvibus** (27) recalls an earlier phrase, **complūribus expugnātīs oppidīs** (1). Good fortune helped the Veneti before; as the Veneti were poised to escape again, what was their bad fortune?
2. What evidence suggests the Veneti believed their fleet invincible? (35–40)
3. Apart from protecting **lēgātī** in the future, what else did Caesar gain in eliminating the Veneti? (40–43)

VOCABULARY REVIEW

aliquis, aliqua, aliquid, *someone, something*
auxilium, -ī, n., *help, aid*
cōgō, -ere, coēgī, coāctus, *to bring together, assemble*
corōna, -ae, f., *garland, wreath*
dīligenter, adv., *carefully*
hōra, -ae, f., *hour*

necō, -āre, -āvī, -ātus, *to kill*
postquam, conj., *after*
quō, adv., *to where, where*
senātus, -ūs, m., *senate*
sōl, sōlis, m., *sun*
terra, -ae, f., *land, ground*
ventus, -ī, m., *wind*

BOOKS IV–V: FAMOUS CROSSINGS

The campaign of 56 ended successfully for Caesar. Brutus had decimated the Venetian fleet, Sabinus won the submission of tribes in Normandy, and Crassus took the chief **oppidum** of the Sontiates in Aquitania. Three years in Gaul had stretched the Roman occupation deep into the mainland and to the coast.

The campaigns of 55 and 54 B.C. are famous for two spectacular crossings, first into Germany, where Caesar pressed local tribes into accepting the Rhine as the **nē plūs ultrā** of German expansion, and then into Britain, where Gallic resistance fighters frequently sought asylum and whose widely rumored natural resources and profitable trade business interested Caesar.

A large exodus of the Usipetes and Tencteri from Germany in 55 drew Caesar to the northern reaches of the Rhine River. The unsettling effect of the migration on the Gallic tribes recalled Ariovistus' incursions years earlier in the south, but to Caesar the German tribes claimed that they had no choice but to migrate, since they were being forced out by the excessive belligerence of the Suebi in Germany. Seeing through this and other attempts at prevarication, one morning Caesar detained the German chiefs in the Roman camp and mounted a blitzkrieg on their camp; most of the 430,000 men, women, and children were killed, but not one Roman died in combat according to Caesar.

> With the German war concluded, Caesar decided that he must cross the Rhine. Several reasons prompted him. The strongest was that he could see the Germans were all too ready to cross into Gaul, and he wanted them to have reasons of their own for anxiety when they realized that an army of the Roman people could and would cross the Rhine. Caesar, *De bello Gallico*, IV.16

Caesar's construction of a bridge over the Rhine in ten days was a remarkable feat of engineering but the crossing turned out to be more symbolic than eventful. One tribe, the Sugambri, who had haughtily replied that "the Rhine was the limit of Roman power," abandoned its villages and fled into the forests. Another tribe, the Ubii, faithful allies of Rome, was assured of a quick Roman return if it should ever again be harassed by the Suebi. After 18 days in Germany, Caesar returned to Gaul and destroyed the bridge, his penchant for dazzling speed intact.

In 55 and again in 54 Caesar crossed the Channel to Britain. On the first crossing he and his men were unprepared for the unforeseen. Inhospitable landing conditions offered little protection against British cavalrymen who effectively fought back their attempts to land (only Caesar's clever use of his warships, which were run ashore at fast speed as amphibious units, and his superior numbers saved the landing) and an unaccustomed high tide destroyed or damaged many of the ships. Short of grain, supplies, and men, Caesar relied on speed and his disciplined troops to blunt the attacks and finally win hostages and a return to Gaul.

Over the winter of 54 Caesar ordered the construction of some 600 ships as part of a larger expeditionary force to Britain. This time, a coalition of coastal and inland tribes led by the warring king Cassivellaunus fiercely contested the Roman invasion. Flash fighting at the Roman camp and on forays inland was not decisive; but when Caesar successfully besieged the king's **oppidum** and the men at the camp strongly beat back a joint force from Kent, Cassivellaunus surrendered. Caesar returned to Gaul with hostages and a promise of annual tribute from Britain.

A poor harvest on the mainland, however, forced Caesar to alter his customary winter quartering. He ordered that six winter camps be fortified within a hundred miles of each other in northern Gaul. Ironically, his own strategy of divide and conquer could now be used against him.

One legion supported by five additional cohorts was assigned to Quintus Sabinus and Lucius Cotta. They were quartered in the land of the Eburones, whose chieftain, Ambiorix, was in league with Indutiomarus of the Treveri. Together they had planned to destroy the quartered legions one by one and unite the opposition under them. In a conference with Roman interpreters, Ambiorix sent the following message—the first part of his master plan—to Sabinus:

> I urge and implore Sabinus, as one with whom I have ties of hospitality, to think of his own safety and that of his soldiers. A large force of German mercenaries has crossed the Rhine and will be here in two days. It is for the Roman generals themselves to decide whether to withdraw their troops from the camp before the neighboring tribes can realize what is happening, and take them to Cicero's camp, about 50 miles away, or to that of Labienus, which is slightly farther.
>
> I promise on my solemn oath that I will give them safe conduct through my territory. In doing so, of course, I am acting in the interests of my tribe by relieving them of the burden of having a Roman winter camp in their territory, and at the same time repaying Caesar for his kindness to me.
>
> Caesar, *De bello Gallico*, V.27

The legates Cotta and Sabinus took opposite sides of the ensuing debate. Cotta argued that they should not abandon camp without direct order from Caesar and that with their grain supply and strong defense they could hold off the Germans until support arrived. Sabinus insisted that by staying they were giving the Germans and Gauls a chance to cut them off from the other camps and starve them to death in a long siege. They argued late into the night until Sabinus bullied the officers and finally Cotta into agreeing to leave camp the next morning under the promise of safe passage from Ambiorix.

1 **Prōnūniātur ... itūrōs**: translate the main verb impersonally and supply **eōs**, the soldiers in the camp, as the subject of **itūrōs** in the indirect statement. The use of the present tense (called historical present) in lines 1–7 and of the historical infinitive in lines 15–16 adds immediacy to the action.

   cōnsūmō, cōnsūmere, cōnsūmpsī, cōnsūmptus, *to use up; of time, to pass, spend.*

   vigiliīs: *without sleep.*

2 **circumspiciō, circumspicere, circumspexī, circumspectus**, *to look around; to examine, look over.*

   quid ... , quid (3). . . .: *(to see) what . . . , (and to see) what. . . .*

3 **īnstrūmentum, -ī**, n., *equipment, gear.*

   *hīberna, -ōrum, n. pl., *winter camp, winter quarters.*

   Omnia: *All (the reasons).*

4 **quārē**, adv., *for which reason, why.*

   quārē nec sine perīculō maneātur et ... perīculum (5): another instance of the impersonal use of an intransitive verb: *(both as to) why staying (there) was not without danger and (why) the danger. . . .*

   languor, languōris, m., *exhaustion, weariness.*

   languōre ... et ... vigiliīs (5): *because of . . . ,* ablatives of cause.

5 **ut quibus esset persuāsum** (6): *as (those set out) to whom it had been persuaded (that). . . .* or, more succinctly, *just like men convinced (that). . . .*

   hoste ... homine: i.e., Ambiorix (for background, see page 65).

7 **datum**: supply **esse**.

   longissimō agmine maximīsque impedīmentīs: ablative of accompaniment with **proficīscuntur** (5). Caesar frequently omits **cum** in this construction when a verb of motion is used in military phrases.

8 **posteā quam**, conj., *after.*

   fremitus, -ūs, m., *uproar, noise.*

9 **profectiō, profectiōnis*, f., *setting out, departure.*

   īnsidiae, -ārum, f. pl., *ambush.*

   bipertītō, adv., *in two parts, at two (different) places.*

   bipertītō in silvīs: as it will soon be clear to the Romans, the Gauls have set up their ambush in the woods at two locations, one, alongside the entrance to the valley, the other, at the ascent out of the valley.

10 **opportūnō atque occultō locō**: supply the preposition **in** here and similarly in line 14.

   ā mīlibus passuum circiter duōbus: *about two miles away (from the camp).*

12 **convallis, convallis, convallium**, f., *valley, defile* (a term used for a narrow pass where troops must march closely bunched or in singe file).

   dēmittō, dēmittere, dēmīsī, dēmissus, *to let down;* + **sē**, *to descend.*

   parte: *side.*

   vallēs, vallis, vallium, f., *valley.*

13 **prīmōs**: *the first (men in line), vanguard.*

   ascēnsū: *from climbing (out of the valley).*

14 **inīquus, -a, -um* + dat., *unfavorable (to or for).*

BOOK V

In anticipation of an early departure, packing and bouts of rationalizing fill the night.

31. Prōnūntiātur prīmā lūce itūrōs. Cōnsūmitur vigiliīs reliqua pars 1
noctis, cum sua quisque mīles circumspiceret, quid sēcum portāre 2
posset, quid ex īnstrūmentō hībernōrum relinquere cōgerētur. Omnia 3
excōgitantur, quārē nec sine perīculō maneātur et languōre mīlitum et 4
vigiliīs perīculum augeātur. Prīmā lūce sīc ex castrīs proficīscuntur ut 5
quibus esset persuāsum nōn ab hoste, sed ab homine amīcissimō 6
cōnsilium datum, longissimō agmine maximīsque impedīmentīs. 7
32. At hostēs, posteā quam ex nocturnō fremitū vigiliīsque dē 8
profectiōne eōrum sēnsērunt, collocātīs īnsidiīs bipertītō in silvīs 9
opportūnō atque occultō locō ā mīlibus passuum circiter duōbus 10
Rōmānōrum adventum exspectābant, et cum sē maior pars agminis in 11
magnam convallem dēmīsisset, ex utrāque parte eius vallis subitō sē 12
ostendērunt novissimōsque premere et prīmōs prohibēre ascēnsū atque 13
inīquissimō nostrīs locō proelium committere coepērunt. 14

Comprehension Questions

1. Caesar often tells us that discipline, experience, and Roman know-how overcome great odds; in their absence, the physical strength, natural cunning, and greater numbers of the enemy prevail. That is the lesson of this tragic episode. Why do the preoccupation with possessions (**sua**, 2) and self-doubt (3–5) foreshadow a breakdown in the ranks?
2. Where was the ambush? What mistakes do we become painfully aware of in the distribution of the marching column and route of the march? (7–14)
3. Where in lines 13–14 is there alliteration and what does it highlight?

VOCABULARY REVIEW
---

amīcus, -a, -um, *friendly*
augeō, -ēre, auxī, auctus, *to increase*
cōgō, -ere, coēgī, coāctus, *to force*
excōgitō, -āre, -āvī, -ātus, *to think of; to consider thoroughly*
lūx, lūcis, f., *light*
  prīmā lūce, *at dawn*
maior, maior, maius, gen., **maiōris,** *greater*
maneō, -ēre, mānsī, mānsus, *to remain, stay*

maximus, -a, -um, *very large, very great*
nec, conj., *nor, and . . . not*
nocturnus, -a, -um, *nighttime*
ostendō, -ere, ostendī, ostentus, *to present, show, reveal*
portō, -āre, -āvī, -ātus, *to carry, bring, take*
prōnūntiō, -āre, -āvī, -ātus, *to announce, make known*
sentiō, -īre, sēnsī, sēnsus, *to feel;* + **dē** + abl., *to become aware of*

15 ***Titūrius, -ī**, m., *Quintus Titurius Sabinus*.

quī . . . prōvīdisset: *because he had. . . .* , a relative clause of characteristic to express cause or reason.

trepidō, -āre, -āvī, -ātus, *to panic, lose one's self-composure*.

trepidāre et concursāre . . . -que dispōnere: historical infinitives; translate as imperfect indicatives.

16 **haec tamen ipsa timidē atque ut**: a verb is needed, such as *he did*, to sum up all of Sabinus' efforts: *however (he did) even these things timidly and (in such a way) that. . . .*

17 **omnia**: i.e., all his powers of leadership and command.

dēficiō, dēficere, dēfēcī, dēfectus, *to fail, desert*.

quod: *(something) that*.

18 **negōtium, -ī**, n., *operation*.

cōnsilium capere, idiom, *to form a plan, come up with a strategy*.

Cotta, -ae, m., *Lucius Aurunculeius Cotta* (the junior legate at the camp).

quī cōgitāsset . . . fuisset: see note to line 15 for a similar **quī** clause.

cōgitāsset: = **cōgitāvisset**.

19 **ob**, prep. + acc., *on account of, due to, for*.

auctor, auctōris, m., *originator, sponsor*; with adjectival force, *in favor (of)*.

20 **nūllā in rē . . . dēerat**: *in no way did he fail (in his responsibility) to. . . .*

21 **imperātōris et . . . mīlitis officia**: to set up the parallel description of Cotta performing both as a commander and as a soldier, take **officia**, the object of **praestābat** (22), first with **imperātōris**, then with **mīlitis**.

22 **minus facile**: with both **obīre** and **prōvidēre** (23).

per sē (23): *by themselves* (i.e., Sabinus and Cotta, who are the subjects of **possent** and **iussērunt**).

23 **obeō, obīre, obiī, obitus**, irreg., *to meet*; + acc., *to take care of*.

quid quōque locō: take **quid** as the subject of **faciendum esset**, and treat **quō locō** as equal in sense to **ubi**.

24 **prōnūntiārī ut**: *that all the soldiers be told to. . . .*; lit., *that it be announced (to all) that. . . .*

orbis, orbis, orbium, f., *circle*.

in orbem cōnsistere, idiom, *to form a defensive circle*.

25 **etsī**, conj., *although*.

eius modī: *of this kind*.

26 **incommodē**, adv., *inconveniently; unfortunately, badly*.

minuit . . . effēcit (27) **. . . vidēbātur** (28): the subject of all three verbs is **id** (29), *it* or *this action*, namely, that of forming into a defensive circle.

27 **alacer, alacris, alacre**, *eager, keen, fired up*.

28 **factum**: supply **esse**.

accidit, quod fierī necesse erat, ut. . . . : (29): *it happened, as expected, that. . . .* ; lit., *it happened, what was necessary to happen, that. . . .* The tragic and quick dissolution of the troops will now be documented and emphasized by asyndeton.

30 **properō, -āre, -āvī, -ātus**, *to hurry, hasten, rush*.

quae (29) **quisque eōrum . . . habēret, . . . properāret**: *(and) what each of them considered* (lit., *held*) *. . . , he rushed. . . .*

31 **flētus, -ūs**, m., *crying, weeping*.

The two commanding legates respond differently to the ambush.

33. Tum dēmum Titūrius, quī nihil ante prōvīdisset, trepidāre et 15
concursāre cohortēsque dispōnere, haec tamen ipsa timidē atque ut eum 16
omnia dēficere vidērentur; quod plērumque eīs accidere cōnsuēvit, quī 17
in ipsō negōtiō cōnsilium capere cōguntur. At Cotta, quī cōgitāsset haec 18
posse in itinere accidere atque ob eam causam profectiōnis auctor nōn 19
fuisset, nūllā in rē commūnī salūtī dēerat et in appellandīs 20
cohortandīsque mīlitibus imperātōris et in pugnā mīlitis officia 21
praestābat. Cum propter longitūdinem agminis minus facile omnia per 22
sē obīre et, quid quōque locō faciendum esset, prōvidēre possent, 23
iussērunt prōnūntiārī ut impedīmenta relinquerent atque in orbem 24
cōnsisterent. Quod cōnsilium etsī in eius modī cāsū reprehendendum 25
nōn est, tamen incommodē accidit: nam et nostrīs mīlitibus spem minuit 26
et hostēs ad pugnam alacriōrēs effēcit, quod nōn sine summō timōre et 27
dēspērātiōne id factum vidēbātur. Praetereā accidit, quod fierī necesse 28
erat, ut vulgō mīlitēs ab signīs discēderent, quae quisque eōrum 29
cārissima habēret, ab impedīmentīs petere atque arripere properāret, 30
clāmōre et flētū omnia complērentur. 31

Comprehension Questions

1. How do Sabinus negatively and Cotta positively remind us of what a good commander should have done in this situation? (15–22)
2. In theory, forming a defensive circle was a good idea, in practice, it failed. Why? (22–28) Compare this failure to Caesar's successful **orbis** on page 47.
3. Lines 28–31 report a significant breakdown of military discipline. Why does Caesar say that it was expected (**quod fierī necesse erat**)? (28–29)

VOCABULARY REVIEW

accidō, -ere, accidī, *to fall down*
accidit, *it happens*
arripiō, -ere, arripuī, arreptus, *to grab, clutch, seize*
cārus, -a, -um, *dear, valuable*
clāmor, clāmōris, m., *shout, shouting*
compleō, -ēre, complēvī, complētus, *to fill*
concursō, -āre, -āvī, -ātus, *to run about*
dēspērātiō, dēspērātiōnis, f., *desperation*

dispōnō, -ere, disposuī, dispositus, *to place here and there; to station, arrange*
efficiō, -ere, effēcī, effectus, *to bring about, make*
longitūdō, longitūdinis, f., *length*
minuō, -ere, minuī, minūtus, *to diminish, lessen, lower*
necesse, indecl. adj., *necessary*
prōvideō, -ēre, prōvīdī, prōvīsus, *to foresee, anticipate*
reprehendō, -ere, reprehendī, reprehēnsus, *to blame, criticize*

32   **permoveō, permovēre, permōvī, permōtus,** *to move deeply; to alarm.*
    ***Ambiorix, Ambiorigis,** m., *Ambiorix* (leader of the Eburones).

33   **interpres, interpretis,** m., *interpreter, translator.*
    Cn. Pompeius, -ī, m., *Gnaeus Pompeius* (possibly a freedman from Gaul who owed his name and position to Pompey the Great).

34   **rogātum:** *to ask.* The accusative of the supine may be used with a verb of motion (implied in **mittit**) to express purpose.
    sibi . . . parcat: the reflexive pronoun refers to Sabinus; the subject of the verb is Ambiorix.
    sī velit sēcum colloquī, licēre (35): part of the indirect statement introduced by **respondit** and continuing to **interpōnere** (37). Sabinus is the subject of **velit** (**vīs** in direct speech), **sēcum** refers to Ambiorix, and **licēre** (with **eī** understood) is impersonal.

35   **spērāre . . . impetrārī posse, quod . . . pertineat** (36): *(that) he* (Ambiorix) *hopes that the request can receive a favorable response . . . , in so far as it concerns* (lit., *which concerns*). . . . The relative clause is the true subject of **posse;** lit., *he hopes that what concerns . . . can be granted.*
    ā multitūdine: *by the majority (of his men),* as if Ambiorix were giving the power of decision to his warriors.
    ***impetrō, -āre, -āvī, -ātus,** *to gain a request, get one's wish.*

36   **pertineō, pertinēre, pertinuī** + **ad** + acc., *to pertain to, concern.*
    ipsī vērō nihil nocitum īrī: *(but Ambiorix assures Sabinus) that no harm, however, will come to him* (i.e., at the meeting), a rare instance of the future passive infinitive, which is formed by joining the supine in **-um** with **īrī,** the present passive infinitive of **eō, īre.**

37   **interpōnō, interpōnere, interposuī, interpositus,** *to place among.*
    fidem interpōnere + **in** + acc., idiom, *to give one's word on.*
    Ille: standing outside the indirect statement and referring to Sabinus.
    saucius, -a, -um, *wounded.*
    commūnicō, -āre, -āvī, -ātus, *to communicate;* + **ut** + subjn., *to discuss the possibility that.*
    sī videātur (38): *if it seems (appropriate),* the usual meaning of **vidērī** when it is not used with an infinitive or complement.

39   **spērāre ab eō. . . .:** *(saying that) from him* (Ambiorix) *he hopes (that).* . . . Sabinus is mimicing Ambiorix' words. For **impetrārī posse,** see note to line 35 above.
    dē suā ac. . . .: *(both) for their own and.* . . . What noun is understood with **suā?**

40   **negō, -āre, -āvī, -ātus,** *to deny; to say that . . . not.*
    in eō: i.e., in his decision.

Abandoned by luck and their leader, as Caesar tells us in paragraphs 34–35, the Roman cohorts began to act independently by charging out of the circle at the Gauls. Ambiorix, the Gallic chieftain, ordered his men in direct line of the Romans to retreat while he ordered others to hurl weapons and keep the Romans from returning to the circle. From dawn to two o'clock the fighting intensified. Leading centurions were killed or wounded, including Cotta who received a serious wound to the face. Sabinus now seeks a truce.

36. Hīs rēbus permōtus Q. Titūrius, cum procul Ambiorigem suōs ⁣ **32**
cohortantem cōnspexisset, interpretem suum Cn. Pompeium ad eum **33**
mittit rogātum ut sibi mīlitibusque parcat. Ille appellātus respondit: sī **34**
velit sēcum colloquī, licēre; spērāre ā multitūdine impetrārī posse, quod **35**
ad mīlitum salūtem pertineat; ipsī vērō nihil nocitum īrī, inque eam rem **36**
sē suam fidem interpōnere. Ille cum Cottā sauciō commūnicat, sī **37**
videātur, pugnā ut excēdant et cum Ambiorige ūnā colloquantur: **38**
spērāre ab eō dē suā ac mīlitum salūte impetrārī posse. Cotta sē ad **39**
armātum hostem itūrum negat atque in eō persevērat. **40**

Comprehension Questions

1. With what request did Sabinus send his translator, Pompeius? (32–34)
2. What was Ambiorix' immediate response? What pledge did he give to Sabinus? Why should Sabinus have been distrustful? (34–37)
2. Against the backdrop of deceit, broken promises, and desperate fighting, how does Caesar discredit Sabinus even further in lines 37–40? In your answer, examine Caesar's use and placement of words such as **sauciō, pugnā** (note the placement), **cum . . . ūnā colloquantur, spērāre,** and **armātum hostem.**
3. Why does Cotta refuse to attend a meeting with Ambiorix? What catastrophe do the words **armātum hostem** foreshadow? (39–40)

VOCABULARY REVIEW

colloquor, -ī, collocūtus sum, *to speak, confer*
fidēs, fideī, f., *good faith, trust*
parcō, -ere, pepercī + dat., *to spare*

persevērō, -āre, -āvī, -ātūrus, *to persevere, persist*
rogō, -āre, -āvī, -ātus, *to ask*
ūnā, adv., *together*

41   **quōs . . . tribūnōs mīlitum . . . habēbat**: the antecedent of the relative clause, **tribūnōs mīlitum**, is contained within the clause in Latin but should precede it in your translation.

      in praesentiā: *for the present, at that moment.*

42   **propius Ambiorigem (43)**: *nearer to Ambiorix.*

43   **imperātum, -ī**, n., *command, order.*

      imperātum facere, idiom, *to execute an order; to obey a command.*

44   **idem**: note the short *i*. What gender, case, and number is **idem**?

      agō, agere, ēgī, āctus + dē + abl., *to discuss, go over.*

45   **cōnsultō**, adv., *on purpose, intentionally.*

      īnstituō, īnstituere, īnstituī, īnstitūtus, *to set up; to initiate, enter upon.*

      sermō, sermōnis, m., *talk, discussion.*

46   **circumventus interficitur**: Sabinus is the subject.

      suō mōre: *by their custom = as was their custom.*

47   **ululātus, -ūs**, m., *howl, shout.*

      ululātum tollere, *to raise a shout; to let out a battle cry.*

49   **L. Petrosidius, -ī**, m., *Lucius Petrosidius.*

      aquilifer, aquiliferī, m., *standard bearer* (the individual who carried the legion's eagle).

50   **aquila, -ae**, f., *eagle;* military, *standard of the legion.*

51   **Illī**: i.e., the Romans who retreated to the camp.

      aegrē, adv., *with difficulty.*

      ad noctem (52): *until nightfall.*

52   **oppugnātiō, oppugnātiōnis**, f., *assault, attack, siege.*

      ad ūnum: *to the last man;* lit., *to a man.*

55   **rēs gestae, rērum gestārum**, f. pl., *achievements; exploits, events.*

   *certiōrem facere, idiom, *to inform.*

Statue of the Gallic chieftain Ambiorix

The meeting with Ambiorix ends horrifically. The Roman legion is over-whelmed.

37. Sabīnus quōs in praesentiā tribūnōs mīlitum circum sē habēbat et 41
prīmōrum ōrdinum centuriōnēs sē sequī iubet et, cum propius 42
Ambiorigem accessisset, iussus arma abicere imperātum facit suīsque ut 43
idem faciant imperat. Interim, dum dē condiciōnibus inter sē agunt 44
longiorque cōnsultō ab Ambiorige īnstituitur sermō, paulātim 45
circumventus interficitur. Tum vērō suō mōre victōriam conclāmant 46
atque ululātum tollunt impetūque in nostrōs factō ōrdinēs perturbant. 47
Ibi L. Cotta pugnāns interficitur cum maximā parte mīlitum. Reliquī sē 48
in castra recipiunt unde erant ēgressī. Ex quibus L. Petrosidius aquilifer, 49
cum magnā multitūdine hostium premerētur, aquilam intrā vāllum 50
prōiēcit; ipse prō castrīs fortissimē pugnāns occīditur. Illī aegrē ad 51
noctem oppugnātiōnem sustinent; noctū ad ūnum omnēs dēspērātā 52
salūte sē ipsī interficiunt. Paucī ex proeliō lāpsī incertīs itineribus per 53
silvās ad T. Labiēnum lēgātum in hīberna perveniunt atque eum dē 54
rēbus gestīs certiōrem faciunt. 55

Caesar, *De bello Gallico* V.31–37

Comprehension Questions

1. Who went with Sabinus to parley with Ambiorix? In what capacity were they attending the meeting? Immediately after arriving how were they compromised? (41–44)
2. How did each of the lieutenants die? What is telling about the manner of their individual deaths? (44–48)
3. No disgrace exceeded the loss of the legion's eagle to the enemy. With heroics at a minimum in this episode, what has L. Petrosidius done that Caesar wishes to immortalize? (49–51)
4. It is unclear whether **sē ipsī interficiunt** represents mass suicide or a mercy killing of each other; in either scenario, what possibly drove them to this? (51–53)

VOCABULARY REVIEW
---

abiciō, -ere, abiēcī, abiectus, *to throw away, throw down*
circum, prep. + acc., *around*
conclāmō, -āre, -āvī, -ātus, *to shout, yell out, raise a cry of*
ēgredior, -ī, ēgressus sum, *to go out, leave, set out*
incertus, -a, -um, *uncertain*

lābor, -ī, lāpsus sum, *to slip away*
mōs, mōris, m., *custom, practice*
prōiciō, -ere, prōiēcī, prōiectus, *to throw forward, throw*
tollō, -ere, sustulī, sublātus, *to lift, raise*
victōria, -ae, f., *victory*

BOOK VII: A NATIONAL UPRISING

The winter revolts, the devastating loss of one and a half legions, and the disappearance of Ambiorix dictated Caesar's strategy for the 53 campaign. He levied more troops and punished the tribes that participated in the revolts. Only Ambiorix eluded him.

Efforts to undermine the Roman occupation of Gaul had so far failed because no tribe or individual had marshalled the numerically superior Gallic forces effectively. The resistance, sporadic at best, had stayed at a regional level.

In the winter and spring of 52, however, conditions were ripe for a national uprising. Rumor of political turmoil in Rome had fostered the belief that Caesar would be detained in Italy, leaving his Gallic legions without leadership. A tribe in the north seized this opportunity to slaughter Roman citizens in the town of Orleans. News of this flagrant assault electrified the Gauls. Many tribes rallied around the chieftain Vercingetorix, who had usurped the throne of his tribe, the Arverni, with an army of beggars and outcasts. Spreading the message of revolution, he sealed the involvement of new tribes by taking hostages and demanding troops and weapons from them. Caesar describes Vercingetorix as follows:

> He was a man of enormous energy, but also a very strict disciplinarian: the severity of his punishments compelled any who were hesitating to obey. Anyone guilty of a serious crime was put to death at the stake or tortured to death; anyone guilty of a lesser crime was sent back home with his ears cut off or a single eye gouged out, to be a warning to others and frighten them by the severity of the punishment. By these savage means he quickly got an army together.
>
> Caesar, *De bello Gallico*, VII.4–5

After losing two well-fortified towns to Caesar and seeing his Gallic cavalry badly beaten by superior German horsemen in Caesar's service, Vercingetorix realized that the Gauls could not hope to win in pitched battles against the better trained Romans. He decided on a strategy that would force the Romans out of Gaul by attrition: a scorched earth policy (burning towns and farming villages to remove sources of supplies and food for the Romans) combined with guerilla warfare aimed at Roman foraging parties.

When Vercingetorix reluctantly spared the town of Bourges, the beautiful and nearly impregnable home of the Bituriges, Caesar attempted a difficult but ultimately successful siege; of the 40,000 men, women, and children in the town, only 800 survived the brute force of the Romans. From there, Caesar tried to take Gergovia, the chief city of the Arverni, but he withdrew after heavy losses. Moreover, new developments were threatening his supply route: the Aedui had overturned a long tradition of pro-Roman support to join the Gallic revolt and Caesar learned that Vercingetorix was planning to use his cavalry to cut off roads to the Province and Italy.

Caesar sent for more German cavalry and cleverly substituted superior Roman horses for their native ones. Vercingetorix abandoned his guerilla tactics and sent his cavalry into battle, convinced that the Roman cavalry would buckle and that the infantry in panic would give up the baggage train. Caesar formed an **orbis** to protect the baggage and his disguised German cavalry upset the Gauls.

Vercingetorix with 80,000 troops retreated to the fortress of Alesia:

> The actual **oppidum** of Alesia was on a hill top, its position being so high that it was clearly impregnable except by blockade. At the bottom, the hill was washed by rivers on two sides. In front of the **oppidum** was a plain about three miles long; on all other sides it was closely surrounded by hills about as high as that on which it stood. The Gallic troops had occupied the whole of the eastern slope of the hill below the wall of the **oppidum**, fortifying their position with a ditch and a six-foot wall.
>
> Caesar, *De bello Gallico*, VII.69

From Alesia Vercingetorix sent messengers to all parts of Gaul demanding that the allied tribes send massive reinforcements to entrap the Romans. In order to succeed, Caesar had to blockade those within Alesia and devise a means of repelling the relief force when it arrived. He began by building a rampart and palisade 12 feet high and 11 miles around behind deep trenches. Lookout towers were placed at 80 foot intervals and forked branches were installed at the base of the palisades to prevent scaling. Additional traps were added: to impale attackers, pointed branches were dug into long trenches and, in front of them, shallow pits with sharp stakes were concealed with brush; also, wood blocks with iron hooks were planted here and there to slow down the assault.

> When these defence works were finished, he constructed another line of fortifications of the same kind, but different from the first in being directed against the enemy on the outside. This second line formed a circuit of 14 miles and followed the most level ground we could find. It was intended to prevent the garrisons in our siegeworks being surrounded, however large a force came against us.
>
> Caesar, *De bello Gallico*, VII.74

More than a month passed before the relief force of nearly 250,000 men and cavalry arrived to save those within Alesia, who were at the point of starvation. Twice the Gauls in Alesia and the relief force from outside coordinated their attacks on the inner and outer rings, and they used dirt and wicker-work to cross the trenches. Many fell victim to the hidden traps and the rest were beaten back by the Romans and German cavalry. A weakness in the Roman defense was then found on the north side of Alesia. There Caesar had built a camp on the lower slopes of a hill that was too large to include in the outer defense wall and he had assigned two legions to it. An elite force of 60,000 Gauls was assembled to penetrate the Roman defense at the camp walls.

> The Arvernian Vercassivellaunus, one of their four chief commanders and a relative of Vercingetorix, was put in command of this force. He left camp soon after sunset and had almost completed his march before dawn. He concealed his men behind the hill, telling them to rest after that night's hard work. When he could see that it was almost midday, he marched towards that camp of ours described above. At the same time, the Gallic cavalry began to advance towards our fortifications in the plain and the rest of their forces appeared in front of their camp.
>
> Caesar, *De bello Gallico*, VII.83

1 *Vercingetorix, Vercingetorigis, m., *Vercingetorix.*
arx, arcis, arcium, f., *citadel, stronghold.*
Alesia, -ae, f., *Alesia.*
suōs: i.e., the Gallic relief force that has taken the field again.

2 *crātis, crātis, crātium, f., *wicker-work* (made from branches and twigs).
mūsculus, -ī, m., (dim. of mūs, *mouse*) *little mouse;* military, *covered shed* (on wheels).

4 quae ... pars: *the side that.* . . .

5 manus, -ūs, f., *hand;* here, *band* (of men), *force, manpower.*
distineō, distinēre, distinuī, distentus, *to keep apart;* pass., *to be spread thin.*

6 occurrit: *it* (i.e., manus) *opposes (the enemy).*
post tergum (7): *from behind.* The idioms *ā tergō and *post tergum mean *in the rear, from behind.*

7 aliēnus, -a, -um, *belonging to another, another's, someone else's.*

8 cōnstō, cōnstāre, cōnstitī, cōnstātūrus, *to rely on, depend on.*
suum perīculum ... cōnstāre: the Romans facing Alesia were relying on the Romans facing the Gallic relief forces not to cave in, and vice-versa. Translate perīculum here as *survival of this danger = safety.*
omnia ... perturbant (9): a generalization, noting that humans exaggerate the meaning of what is not clearly at hand; abesse = *to be out of sight.*

10 idōneus, -a, -um, *suitable.*
idōneum locum: perhaps on Mt. de Flavigny, from where Caesar could observe and direct all the operations; consult the map on page 78.
quid quāque in parte gerātur: see page 68, line 23 for a similar expression.

11 Utrīsque ad animum occurrit: *It occurs to each side (that).* . . .

12 quō: ablative of time when, but in line 15 quō is adverbial, *where.*
contendī conveniat: note the impersonal verbs here and again in line 15.

13 perfringō, perfringere, perfrēgī, perfrāctus, *to break through.*

14 obtineō, obtinēre, obtinuī, obtentus + rem, *to hold one's position.*
maximē ... labōrātur (15): i.e., at the Roman camp under Mt. Rea.

15 *Vercassivellaunus, -ī, m., *Vercassivellaunus* (one of four generals in charge of the relief forces, from the tribe of the Arverni).
*dēmōnstrō, -āre, -āvī, -ātus, *to point out; to explain; to state, mention.*

16 dēclīvitās, dēclīvitātis, f., *descent.*
fastīgium, -ī, n., *slope.*
mōmentum, -ī, n., *movement; influence, factor.*
Inīquum ... fastīgium magnum habet mōmentum: *the Gauls use the uneven slope . . . to their great advantage* (i.e., downward momentum); lit., *the uneven slope . . . has a great influence.*

17 testūdō, testūdinis, f., *turtle;* military, *turtle shell formation* (made here by overlaying shields in front of the troop mass and overhead).
in vicem, adv., *in turn.*
*integrī, -ōrum, m. pl., *fresh troops.*

18 succēdō, succēdere, successī, successūrus, *to come up;* + dat., *to relieve.*

19 occultō, -āre, -āvī, -ātus, *to hide, conceal.*
contegō, contegere, contēxī, contēctus, *to cover up.*

20 suppetō, suppetere, supetīvī, *to be available; to hold out.*

BOOK VII

A coordinated Gallic assault on the outer and inner ring launches the final and most desperate fighting of the siege.

84. Vercingetorix ex arce Alesiae suōs cōnspicātus ex oppidō 1
ēgreditur; crātēs, longuriōs, mūsculōs, falcēs reliquaque, quae ēruptiōnis 2
causā parāverat, prōfert. Pugnātur ūnō tempore omnibus locīs atque 3
omnia temptantur; quae minimē vīsa pars fīrma est, hūc concurritur. 4
Rōmānōrum manus tantīs mūnītiōnibus distinētur nec facile plūribus 5
locīs occurrit. Multum ad terrendōs nostrōs valet clāmor, quī post 6
tergum pugnantibus exstitit, quod suum perīculum in aliēnā vident 7
virtūte cōnstāre; omnia enim plērumque quae absunt vehementius 8
hominum mentēs perturbant. 9
85. Caesar idōneum locum nactus, quid quāque in parte gerātur, 10
cognōscit, labōrantibus summittit. Utrīsque ad animum occurrit ūnum 11
esse illud tempus quō maximē contendī conveniat: Gallī, nisi 12
perfrēgerint mūnītiōnēs, dē omnī salūte dēspērant; Rōmānī, sī rem 13
obtinuerint, fīnem labōrum omnium exspectant. Maximē ad superiōrēs 14
mūnītiōnēs labōrātur, quō Vercassivellaunum missum dēmōnstrāvimus. 15
Inīquum locī ad dēclīvitātem fastīgium magnum habet mōmentum. Aliī 16
tēla coniciunt, aliī testūdine factā subeunt; dēfatīgātīs in vicem integrī 17
succēdunt. Agger ab ūniversīs in mūnītiōnem coniectus et ascēnsum 18
dat Gallīs et ea, quae in terrā occultāverant Rōmānī, contegit; nec iam 19
arma nostrīs nec vīrēs suppetunt. 20

Comprehension Questions

1. What tools were collected for the assault? What was their purpose? (1–3)
2. Where were the Gauls having the most success and why? (3–9)
3. Where was Caesar? What was his role at this stage of the battle? (10–11)
4. In the balance was the future of Gaul and the reward of seven years of fighting. What does Caesar imagine each side is thinking? (11–14)
5. How did Vercassivellaunus neutralize the fortifications and the hidden traps to threaten the defensive integrity of the Roman camp? (14–20)

VOCABULARY REVIEW

hūc, adv., *to this place, here*
multum, adv., *very, especially*
parō, -āre, -āvī, -ātus, *to prepare*
plūrēs, plūrēs, plūra, gen. pl.,
  plūrium, *more, several*

prōferō, prōferre, prōtulī,
  prōlātus, irreg., *to bring out*
temptō, -āre, -āvī, -ātus, *to try*
terreō, -ēre, -uī, -itus, *to terrify*

22   **imperat, sī . . . possit, . . . pugnet** (23): Caesar is the subject of the first verb, Labienus of the next two. In indirect commands, the subordinating conjunction **ut** may be left out, as it is here before **pugnet**. The idiom **ēruptiōne pugnāre** means *to fight one's way out.*

23   **id . . . nē faciat:** governed by **imperat; id** refers to **ēruptiōne pugnet.**
    reliquōs: i.e., the Romans protecting the inner ring south of Alesia.

24   **succumbō, succumbere, succubuī, succubitūrus,** *to lie down;* + dat., *to yield (to), give up (on).*
    superiōrum: *earlier.*
    dīmicātiō, dīmicātiōnis, f., *combat, battle.*

25   **frūctus, -ūs,** m., *fruit; reward, payoff.*
    interior, interior, interius, gen., **interiōris,** *inner.*
       interiōrēs: *the Gauls fighting from within;* lit., *those on the inside.*

26   **campester, campestris, campestre,** *of level ground, level.*
       dēspērātīs campestribus locīs: unable to scale the extensive defense-works on the plain, the Gauls will now try to storm the ramparts on the low lying hills south of Alesia.
    praeruptus, -a, -um, *steep.*
       praerupta ex ascēnsū (27): *with a steep incline;* lit., *steep due to its climb.*

28   **prōpugnantēs:** i.e., the Romans in the defensive towers on the wall.
    dēturbō, -āre, -āvī, -ātus, *to drive off* or *back, force back.*

29   **lōrīca, -ae,** f., *leather cuirass;* here, *defensive covering* (on the rampart).
    rescindō, rescindere, rescidī, rescissus, *to cut down, tear down.*

30   **cum cohortibus:** either Caesar did not record how many cohorts went with Brutus or, more likely, an error of omission was made in the manuscripts.

31   **C. Fabius, -ī,** m., *Gaius Fabius.*

34   **equitum partem se sequī, partem circumīre . . . iubet** (35): Caesar divides the cavalry, ordering some to follow him (**sē,** a reflexive pronoun because he is the subject of the main verb), others to circle around back.

35   **exterior, exterior, exterius,** gen., **exteriōris,** *outer.*

39   **accelerō, -āre, -āvī, -ātus,** *to rush, hurry.*
    intersum, interesse, interfuī, irreg. + dat., *to be present at; to take part in.*

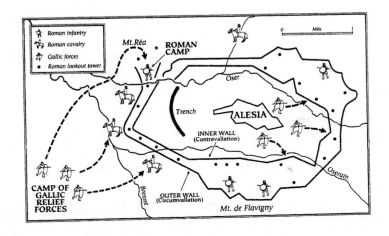

Caesar sends Labienus, Brutus, and Fabius to repulse the fierce assault.

86. Hīs rēbus cognitīs Caesar Labiēnum cum cohortibus sex subsidiō   21
labōrantibus mittit; imperat, sī sustinēre nōn possit, dēductīs cohortibus   22
ēruptiōne pugnet; id nisi necessāriō nē faciat. Ipse adit reliquōs;   23
cohortātur nē labōrī succumbant; omnium superiōrum dīmicātiōnum   24
frūctum in eō diē atque hōrā docet cōnsistere. Interiōrēs dēspērātīs   25
campestribus locīs propter magnitūdinem mūnītiōnum loca praerupta   26
ex ascēnsū temptant; hūc ea quae parāverant cōnferunt. Multitūdine   27
tēlōrum ex turribus prōpugnantēs dēturbant, aggere et crātibus fossās   28
explent, falcibus vāllum ac lōrīcam rescindunt.   29
87. Mittit prīmum Brūtum adulēscentem cum cohortibus Caesar, post   30
cum aliīs C. Fabium lēgātum; postrēmō ipse, cum vehementius   31
pugnārētur, integrōs subsidiō addūcit. Restitūtō proeliō ac repulsīs   32
hostibus eō quō Labiēnum mīserat contendit; cohortēs quattuor ex   33
proximō castellō dēdūcit, equitum partem sē sequī, partem circumīre   34
exteriōrēs mūnītiōnēs et ā tergō hostēs adorīrī iubet. Labiēnus,   35
postquam neque aggerēs neque fossae vim hostium sustinēre poterant,   36
coāctīs ūndecim cohortibus, quās ex proximīs praesidiīs dēductās fors   37
obtulit, Caesarem per nūntiōs facit certiōrem quid faciendum exīstimet.   38
Accelerat Caesar, ut proeliō intersit.   39

Comprehension Questions

1. How many troops were sent to help the Romans on the north side? (21–23)
2. Where did Caesar go and with what purpose? (23–25)
3. Describe the Gallic assault on the walls along the southern slopes. (25–29)
4. What measures did Caesar take to meet this threat to the inner ring? (30–32)
5. How did he intend to help Labienus on the outer ring? If **quid faciendum** (38) refers to the fail-safe option in lines 22–23, what was Labienus planning and why was Caesar rushing to intervene there?

VOCABULARY REVIEW
---

addūcō, -ere, addūxī, adductus,
  to bring along, bring up
adeō, adīre, adiī, aditus, irreg., *to*
  go to, approach
circumeō, circumīre, circumiī,
  circumitus, irreg., *to go*
  around, circle
expleō, -ēre, explēvī, explētus, *to*
  fill up, fill

nūntius, -ī, m., *messenger*
ūndecim, *eleven*
post, adv., *afterwards, next*
postrēmō, adv., *at last, finally*
prōpugnō, -āre, -āvī, -ātus, *to*
  fight for, defend
repellō, -ere, reppulī, repulsus,
  to drive back

40 **ex colōre vestītūs**: Caesar wore a scarlet military cloak into combat.
    īnsigne, īnsignis, īnsignium, n., *distinguishing dress.*
41 **cōnsuērat**: contracted from **cōnsuēverat**.
    turma, -ae, f., *troop, squadron* (of cavalry).
42 **dēvexus, -a, -um**, *sloping, descending.*
    ut . . . haec dēclīvia et dēvexa: substantive use of the neuter adjectives:
    since these slopes and descents. . . . Caesar explains why the Gauls higher
    up on Mt. Rea (**dē locīs superiōribus**) were able to see Caesar and his
    reserves descending from Mt. de Flavigny.
    *cernō, cernere, crēvī, crētus, *to distinguish; to spot, see.*
43 **utrimque**, adv., *from both sides.*
    excipiō, excipere, excēpī, exceptus, *to receive; to follow, succeed.*
    clāmōre sublātō excipit rūrsus . . . clāmor (44): *after the first round of
    shouts was taken up, a second round followed.* The first shouts came from
    the site of the renewed fighting, the second from all the rest.
44 **omittō, omittere, omīsī, omissus**, *to let go of; to throw aside.*
47 ***caedēs, caedis, caedium**, f., *killing, slaughter.*
    Sedulius, -ī, m., *Sedulius.*
    Lemovīcēs, Lemovīcum, m. pl., *Lemovices* (a Gallic tribe living west of the
    Arverni in central Gaul).
48 ***Arvernus, -a, -um**, *of the Arverni, Arvernian*; m. pl., *the Arverni* (a powerful
    tribe from central Gaul, home of Vercingetorix).
49 **paucī . . . recipiunt (50)**: referring here and in line 52 to the relief force.
50 **Cōnspicātī ex oppidō . . .** : *When (the leaders) from the town saw. . . .*
52 **prōtinus**, adv., *at once, immediately.*
53 **dēfetīscor, dēfetīscī, dēfessus sum**, *to become worn out.*
    Quod nisi (52) . . . essent dēfessī, . . . dēlērī potuissent (54): *But if
    (they) had not been worn out . . . , (they) could have been destroyed,* a past
    contrary to fact condition.

Statue of the dying Gaul

The final confrontation begins.

88. Eius adventū ex colōre vestītūs cognitō, quō īnsignī in proeliīs ūtī 40
cōnsuērat, turmīsque equitum et cohortibus vīsīs, quās sē sequī 41
iusserat, ut dē locīs superiōribus haec dēclīvia et dēvexa cernēbantur, 42
hostēs proelium committunt. Utrimque clāmōre sublātō excipit rūrsus 43
ex vāllō atque omnibus mūnītiōnibus clāmor. Nostrī, omissīs pīlīs, 44
gladiīs rem gerunt. Repente post tergum equitātus cernitur; cohortēs 45
aliae appropinquant. Hostēs terga vertunt; fugientibus equitēs 46
occurrunt. Fit magna caedēs. Sedulius, dux et prīnceps Lemovīcum, 47
occīditur; Vercassivellaunus Arvernus vīvus in fugā comprehenditur; 48
signa mīlitāria septuāgintā quattuor ad Caesarem referuntur; paucī ex 49
tantō numerō sē incolumēs in castra recipiunt. Cōnspicātī ex oppidō 50
caedem et fugam suōrum dēspērātā salūte cōpiās ā mūnītiōnibus 51
redūcunt. Fit prōtinus hāc rē audītā ex castrīs Gallōrum fuga. Quod nisi 52
crēbrīs subsidiīs ac tōtius diēī labōre mīlitēs essent dēfessī, omnēs 53
hostium cōpiae dēlērī potuissent. Dē mediā nocte missus equitātus 54
novissimum agmen cōnsequitur; magnus numerus capitur atque 55
interficitur, reliquī ex fugā in cīvitātēs discēdunt. 56

Comprehension Questions

1. Why was Caesar's arrival so easily detected? What statement of purpose was intended by it? (40–41) Where in earlier battles did his arrival give a psychological boost to his men or turn the direction of the battle?
2. Using his flamboyant entry, the conspicuous arrival of reinforcements, and the focused attention of participants of both sides, Caesar has cleverly masked a final and brilliant surprise; what was it? (40–46)
3. The outcome is tersely recounted; although objective in tone, how does Caesar make us aware of the severity of the Gallic loss through word choice, verb tense, and word order? (45–50)
4. How did those within Alesia and those in the camp of the relief force react to the sight and news of the Roman victory at the wall? (50–52)
5. Why was there not an immediate pursuit of the enemy? When did Caesar send his cavalry in pursuit and with what results? (52–56)

VOCABULARY REVIEW

color, colōris, m., *color*
dux, ducis, m., *leader*
incolumis, -is, -e, *unharmed*
medius, -a, -um, *middle, mid-*
mīlitāris, -is, -e, *military*
prīnceps, prīncipis, m., *leader, chieftain*

redūcō, -ere, redūxī, reductus, *to lead* or *bring back, withdraw*
referō, referre, retulī, relātus, irreg., *to bring back*
septuāgintā, *seventy*
vestītus, -ūs, m., *clothing*
vīvus, -a, -um, *living, alive*

57 concilium, -ī, n., *meeting, assembly.*
58 suscipiō, suscipere, suscēpī, susceptus, *to take up, undertake.*
    necessitās, necessitātis, f., *necessity; advantage, interest.*
59 quoniam . . . velint (60): also part of the indirect statement intoduced by
    dēmōnstrat. Explain why sit and velint are subjunctives.
    cēdō, cēdere, cessī, cessūrus, *to go;* + dat., *to yield (to), submit (to).*
       sit fortūnae cēdendum: *they must submit to fortune;* lit., *submission is to be
          made to fortune.*
    ad utramque rem: *regarding either of two options;* lit., *for each (course of)
       action.*
60 seu . . . seu, conj., *whether . . . or.*
    satisfaciō, satisfacere, satisfēcī, satisfactus, *to satisfy;* + dat., *to please,
       placate, appease.*
    vīvum: eum is understood.
62 cōnsīdō, cōnsīdere, cōnsēdī, *to sit down, sit.*
64 sī . . . posset: *if he could, in the hope that he could.*
    recuperō, -āre, -āvī, -ātus, *to recover, get back; to regain the backing of.*
65 capita singula: *one slave each;* lit., *one head each.*
    praeda, -ae, f., *booty, plunder.*

Vercingetorix surrenders to Caesar

Vercingetorix surrenders.

89. Posterō diē Vercingetorix conciliō convocātō id bellum sē   57
suscēpisse nōn suārum necessitātum sed commūnis lībertātis causā   58
dēmōnstrat, et, quoniam sit fortūnae cēdendum, ad utramque rem sē   59
illīs offerre, seu morte suā Rōmānīs satisfacere seu vīvum trādere velint.   60
Mittuntur dē hīs rēbus ad Caesarem lēgātī. Iubet arma trādī, prīncipēs   61
prōdūcī. Ipse in mūnītiōne prō castrīs cōnsēdit; eō ducēs prōdūcuntur,   62
Vercingetorix dēditur, arma prōiciuntur. Reservātīs Aeduīs atque   63
Arvernīs, sī per eōs cīvitātēs recuperāre posset, ex reliquīs captīvīs tōtī   64
exercituī capita singula praedae nōmine distribuit.   65

Caesar, *De bello Gallico* VII.84–89

Comprehension Questions

1. Before submitting to a decision by his peers, Vercingetorix briefly appeals to what noble cause for his involvement in the revolt of 52 B.C.? (57–58)
2. What choice does Vercingetorix give them? (59–60)
3. The spareness of style recalls Caesar's famous dictum, **Vēnī, vīdī, vīcī.** What are Caesar's terms? What prefix and two verbal roots are concentrated in lines 61–63?
4. Fully aware that in winning at Alesia, he had potentially ended the war and subjugated all of Gaul, how does his treatment of the captives reflect both a desire to settle affairs in Gaul and to ready himself politically and militarily for his next move, that of attending to Pompey and the Senate? (63–65)

VOCABULARY REVIEW

captīvus, -ī, m., *captive, prisoner*
distribuō, -ere, distribuī,
    distribūtus, *to distribute, allot*
lībertās, lībertātis, f., *freedom*
mors, mortis, f., *death*
nōmen, nōminis, n., *name*

posterus, -a, -um, *following, next*
prōdūcō, -ere, prōdūxī,
    prōductus, *to bring (forth)*
quoniam, conj., *since, because*
reservō, -āre, -āvī, -ātus, *to keep*
    back, withhold

VOCABULARY

This vocabulary lists all words that appear in the running vocabularies with asterisks, and all words from the vocabulary review boxes that appear more than once in the text.

A

ā or ab, prep. + abl., *from; by; in, on*
abdō, -ere, abdidī, abditus, *to hide*
absum, abesse, āfuī, āfutūrus, irreg., *to be away*
ac, conj., *and*
accēdō, -ere, accessī, accessūrus, *to advance, go, come*
accipiō, -ere, accēpī, acceptus, *to get, receive*
ācer, ācris, ācre, *fierce*
aciēs, -ēī, f., *battle line*
ad, prep. + acc., *to, toward; at*
adigō, -ere, adēgī, adāctus, *to hurl*
adorior, -īrī, adortus sum, *to attack*
adulēscēns, adulēscentis, *young*
adventus, -ūs, m., *arrival*
adversus, -a, -um, *opposite, facing*
Aeduī, -ōrum, m. pl., *the Aedui*
agger, aggeris, m., *mound; rampart; earth*
agmen, agminis, n., *marching line*
    novissimum agmen, *rear line*
agō, -ere, ēgī, āctus, *to drive; to do*
ālāriī, -ōrum, m. pl., *auxiliary troops*
alius, alia, aliud, *other, another*
    aliī . . . aliī, *some . . . others*
alter, altera, alterum, *the other*
    alter . . . alter, *the one . . . the other*
altitūdō, altitūdinis, f., *height; depth*
Ambiorix, Ambiorigis, m., *Ambiorix*
amīcitia, -ae, f., *friendship*
āmittō, -ere, āmīsī, āmissus, *to lose*
angustiae, -ārum, f. pl., *difficulties*
animadvertō, -ere, animadvertī, animadversus, *to notice*
animus, -ī, m., *mind; spirit, courage*
ante, adv., *earlier, in advance*
antemna, -ae, f., *yardarm*
apertus, -a, -um, *open, exposed, bare*

appellō, -āre, -āvī, -ātus, *to name, call*
appropinquō, -āre, -āvī, *to approach*
Aquītānī, -ōrum, m. pl., *Aquitani*
Arar, Araris, m., *the Saone River*
Ariovistus, -ī, m., *Ariovistus*
arma, -ōrum, n. pl., *arms, weapons*
armātus, -a, -um, *armed*
Arvernī, -ōrum, m. pl., *the Arverni*
ascēnsus, -ūs, m., *climb, approach*
at, conj., *but*
atque, conj., *and*
audeō, -ēre, ausus sum, *to dare*
audiō, -īre, -īvī, -ītus, *to hear*
    dictō audiēns, *obedient*
aut, conj., *or*
    aut . . . aut, *either . . . or*
autem, particle, *but; moreover*
auxilium, -ī, n., *help, aid*

B

barbarus, -a, -um, *foreign;* m. pl., *foreigners, natives*
Belgae, -ārum, m. pl., *the Belgae*
bellum, -ī, n., *war*
brevitās, brevitātis, f., *shortness*
Brutus, -ī, m., *Brutus*

C

caedēs, caedis, caedium, f., *killing, slaughter*
Caesar, Caesaris, m., *Caesar*
cālō, cālōnis, m., *camp servant*
capiō, -ere, cēpī, captus, *to capture*
caput, capitis, n., *head*
Cassius, -ī, m., *Cassius*
castellum, -ī, n., *lookout tower*
castra, -ōrum, n. pl., *camp*
    castra movēre, *to break camp*
cāsus, -ūs, m., *misfortune, disaster*
    cāsū, adv., *by chance, accidentally*

84

causa, -ae, f., *cause, reason*
causā, prep. + preceeding gen., *for the sake of*
celer, celeris, celere, *swift, quick*
celeritās, celeritātis, f., *speed*
cēlō, -āre, -āvī, -ātus, *to hide*
centuriō, centuriōnis, m., *centurion*
cernō, -ere, crēvī, crētus, *to spot, see*
certus, -a, -um, *certain*
certiōrem facere, *to inform*
circiter, adv., *about*
circumveniō, -īre, circumvēnī, circumventus, *to surround*
cīvitās, cīvitātis, f., *state, nation*
clāmor, clāmōris, m., *shout, shouting*
classis, classis, classium, f., *fleet*
claudō, -ere, clausī, clausus, *to shut*
coepī, coepisse, coeptus, defective verb, *I began*
cōgitō, -āre, -āvī, -ātus, *to think*
cognōscō, -ere, cognōvī, cognitus, *to find out, learn*
cōgō, -ere, coēgī, coāctus, *to assemble; to force*
cohors, cohortis, cohortium, f., *cohort*
cohortor, -ārī, cohortātus sum, *to exhort, encourage*
collis, collis, collium, m., *hill*
collocō, -āre, -āvī, -ātus, *to place*
comminus, adv., *hand to hand*
committō, -ere, commīsī, commissus, *to entrust*
committere proelium, *to enter battle, start fighting*
commodē, adv., *adequately*
commoveō, -ēre, commōvī, commōtus, *to alarm*
commūnis, -is, -e, *common*
complūrēs, -ēs, -a, *several, many*
comprehendō, -ere, comprehendī, comprehēnsus, *to catch*
concidō, -ere, concidī, *to fall down*
concurrō, -ere, concurrī, concursūrus, *to rush*
condiciō, condiciōnis, f., *terms*
conferō, conferre, contulī, collātus, irreg., *to bring together, gather*
cōnfertus, -a, -um, *closely packed*
cōnficiō, -ere, cōnfēcī, cōnfectus, *to complete; to exhaust, overcome*
cōnfīdō, -ere, cōnfīsus sum, *to trust*
congredior, congredī, congressus sum, *to come into contact; to fight*
coniciō, -ere, coniēcī, coniectus, *to throw, hurl*
cōnsequor, -ī, cōnsecūtus sum, *to follow after; to overtake*
cōnservō, -āre, -āvī, -ātus, *to save*
cōnsilium, -ī, n., *plan, purpose*
cōnsistō, -ere, cōnstitī, *to take up a position; to depend (on)*
cōnspectus, -ūs, m., *sight*
cōnspiciō, -ere, cōnspexī, cōnspectus, *to catch sight of, notice, see*
cōnspicor, -ārī, cōnspicātus sum, *to catch sight of, notice, see*
cōnstituō, -ere, cōnstituī, cōnstitūtus, *to set up, arrange, place*
cōnsuēscō, -ere, cōnsuēvī, cōnsuētus, *to be accustomed*
cōnsuētūdō, cōnsuētūdinis, f., *custom, habit*
cōnsul, cōnsulis, m., *consul*
contendō, -ere, contendī, contentus, *to fight; to try; to hasten*
contineō, -ēre, continuī, contentus, *to hold, keep*
contrā, prep. + acc., *against*
conveniō, -īre, convēnī, conventus, *to come together; to be agreed upon*
convertō, -ere, convertī, conversus, *to turn (around)*
convocō, -āre, -āvī, -ātus, *to convene*
cōpiae, -ārum, f. pl., *troops*
cornū, -ūs, n., *wing (of an army)*
corpus, corporis, n., *body*
Cotta, -ae, m., *Cotta*
crātis, crātis, cratium, f., *wicker-work*
crēber, crēbra, crēbrum, *numerous*
cum, prep. + abl., *with*
cum, conj., *when; since; although*
cupidus, -a, -um, *desirous, eager*

D

dē, prep. + abl., *down from; about; at the start of; just after*

dēbeō, -ēre, -uī, -itus, *(one) ought*

decimus, -a, -um, *tenth*

dēclīvis, -is, -e, *sloping downward*

dēcurrō, -ere, dē(cu)currī, dēcursus, *to run (down)*

dēditiō, dēditiōnis, f., *surrender*

dēdō, -ere, dēdidī, dēditus, *to give up, surrender*

dēdūcō, -ere, dēdūxī, dēductus, *to withdraw, remove*

dēfatīgō, -āre, -āvī, -ātus, *to wear out, exhaust*

dēfendō, -ere, dēfendī, dēfēnsus, *to defend*

dēiciō, -ere, dēiēcī, dēiectus, *to throw down*

dēleō, -ēre, dēlēvī, dēlētus, *to destroy; to remove*

dēmōnstrō, -āre, -āvī, -ātus, *to explain; to state*

dēmum, adv., *finally, at last*

dēspērō, -āre, -āvī, -ātus + dē + abl., *to lose hope of, give up on*

dēsum dēesse, dēfuī, irreg., *to be lacking; to fail*

dētrahō, -ere, dētrāxī, dētractus, *to take away*

dexter, dextera, dexterum, *right*

dīcō, -ere, dīxī, dictus, *to say*
   dictō audiēns, *obedient*

diēs, diēī, m., *day*

discēdō, -ere, discessī, discessūrus, *to leave, go away*

dīvīsus, -a, -um, *divided*

dō, dare, dedī, datus, *to give*

doceō, -ēre, docuī, doctus, *to teach, instruct, show*

domus, -ūs, abl., **domō,** f., *home*

ducentī, -ae, -a, *two hundred*

dūcō, -ere, dūxī, ductus, *to lead*

dum, conj., *while*

duo, duae, duo, *two*

dux, ducis, m., *leader*

E

ē or **ex,** prep. + abl., *from, out of*

ēdūcō, -ere, ēdūxī, ēductus, *to lead or take (out)*

ēgredior, -ī, ēgressus sum, *to go out, leave, set out*

enim, postpositive conj., *for*

eō, īre, iī, itūrus, irreg., *to go*

eō, adv., *to that place, there*

equitēs, equitum, m. pl., *cavalry*

equitātus, -ūs, m., *cavalry*

ēruptiō, ēruptiōnis, f., *breaking out*

et, conj., *and*
   et . . . et, *both . . . and*

etiam, adv., *also, even*

excēdō, -ere, excessī, excessus, *to go out; to depart, withdraw*

excipiō, -ere, excēpī, exceptus, *to receive, follow, succeed*

exeō, exīre, exiī, exitus, irreg., *to go out, leave*

exercitus, -ūs, m., *army*

exiguitās, exiguitātis, f., *shortage*

exīstimō, -āre, -āvī, -ātus, *to believe*

expedītus, -a, -um, *lightly armed*

expugnō, -āre, -āvī, -ātus, *to take by storm, capture*

exsistō, -ere, exstitī, *to surface, arise*

exspectō, -āre, -āvī, -ātus, *to wait for, expect*

extrēmus, -a, -um, *last, final*

F

facile, adv., *easily*

faciō, -ere, fēcī, factus, *to make, do*
   certiōrem facere, *to inform*
   impetum facere in + acc., *to attack*

factum, -ī, n., *deed*

falx, falcis, falcium, f., *hook*

ferē, adv., *nearly, almost*

ferō, ferre, tulī, lātus, irreg., *to bring; to bear, endure*
   signa ferre, *to advance*

fīnis, fīnis, fīnium, m., *end; boundary;* pl., *borders, territory*

fīnitimī, -ōrum, m. pl., *neighboring tribes*

fīō, fierī, factus sum, irreg., *to be done; to happen*

firmus, -a, -um, *firm, strong*

flūmen, flūminis, n., *river*

fore, alternate form of **futūrus esse**, see **sum**

fors, fortis, f., *luck, chance*

fortis, -is, -e, *strong; brave*

fortūna, -ae, f., *fortune*

fossa, -ae, f., *ditch, trench*

frūmentum, -ī, n., *grain*; pl., *crops*

fuga, -ae, f., *flight*

fugiō, -ere, fūgī, fugitūrus, *to flee, run away*

G

Gallia, -ae, f., *Gaul*

Gallī, -ōrum, m. pl., *the Gauls*

Germānī, -ōrum, m. pl., *the Germans*

gerō, -ere, gessī, gestus, *to conduct*
  rem gerere, *to fight (a battle)*

gladius, -ī, m., *sword*

gravis, -is, -e, *heavy; serious*

H

habeō, -ēre, -uī, -itus, *to have*

Helvētius, -a, -um, *of the Helvetii, Helvetian*; m. pl., *the Helvetii*

hīberna, -ōrum, n. pl., *winter camp*

hic, haec, hoc, *this*

homō, hominis, m., *man, person*

hōra, -ae, f., *hour*

hostis, hostis, hostium, m., *an enemy*; pl., *the enemy*

hūc, adv., *to this place, here*

I

iaciō, -ere, iēcī, iactus, *to throw*

iam, adv., *now, already*

ibi, adv., *in that place, there*

īdem, eadem, idem, *the same*

ille, illa, illud, *that*

impedīmentum, -ī, n., *impediment, obstacle*; pl., *baggage train*

impediō, -īre, -īvī, -ītus, *to hamper*

imperātor, imperātōris, m., *general*

imperō, -āre, -āvi, -ātus, *to order*

impetrō, -āre, -āvī, -ātus, *to gain a request*

impetus, -ūs, m., *attack*
  impetum facere in + acc., *to attack*

in, prep. + acc., *into, onto; against*;
  + abl., *in, on*

incitō, -āre, -āvī, -ātus, *to drive forward*

incolō, -ere, incoluī, *to dwell*

incrēdibilis, -is, -e, *remarkable*

īnferior, īnferior, īnferius, gen., **īnferiōris**, *lower*

īnferō, īnferre, intulī, illātus, irreg., *to bring (in); to inflict*

inīquus, -a, -um, *uneven; unfavorable*

iniūria, -ae, f., *harm, injury*

īnstō, -āre, īnstitī, *to press forward*

īnstruō, -ere, īnstrūxī, īnstrūctus, *to draw up, form*

integrī, -ōrum, m. pl., *fresh troops*

intellegō, -ere, intellēxī, intellēctus, *to understand; to find out, learn*

inter, prep. + acc., *between, among*

interficiō, -ere, interfēcī, interfectus, *to kill*

interim, adv., *meanwhile*

intrā, prep. + acc., *inside, within*

ipse, ipsa, ipsum, *himself, herself, itself, themselves*

is, ea, id, *he, she, it; this, that*

ita, adv., *thus; so*

itaque, conj., *and so, therefore*

item, adv., *likewise, in the same way*

iter, itineris, n., *route; march*

itūrus, from **eō, īre**

iubeō, -ēre, iussī, iussus, *to order*

iūdicō, -āre, -āvī, -ātus, *to decide*

L

Labiēnus, -ī, m., *Labienus*

labor, labōris, m., *work; effort*

labōrō, -āre, -āvī, -ātus, *to work; to struggle, be in trouble*

lateō, -ēre, latuī, *to be concealed*

laus, laudis, f., *praise, acclaim*

lēgātus, -ī, m., *envoy; lieutenant*

legiō, legiōnis, f., *legion*

legiōnārius, -a, -um, *legionary*
licet, -ēre, licuit, *it is permitted*
linter, lintris, f., *canoe*
locus, -ī, m., n. in pl., *place, area, location*
longus, -a, -um, *long*
    longē, adv., *far*
longurius, -ī, m., *long pole*

M

māchinātiō, māchinātiōnis, f., *machine, mechanical device*
magis, adv., *more*
magnitūdō, magnitūdinis, f., *greatness, size*
magnus, -a, -um, *big, large, great*
manus, -ūs, f., *hand*
maximē, adv., *very much, especially*
maximus, -a, -um, *very great , very large*
memoria, -ae, f., *memory*
mēns, mentis, mentium, f., *mind*
mercātor, mercātōris, m., *merchant, trader*
mīles, mīlitis, m., *soldier*
mīlle, indeclinable noun and adjective, *a thousand*
    mīlia, mīlium, n. pl., *thousands*
    mille passūs, *a mile*
minimē, adv., *very little, the least*
minor, minor, minus, gen., minōris, *smaller, less*
minus, adv., *less*
mittō, -ere, mīsī, missus, *to send*
modus, -ī, m., *manner*
moveō, -ēre, mōvī, mōtus, *to move*
    castra movēre, *to break camp*
multī, -ae, -a, *many*
multitūdō, multitūdinis, f., *(large) number, (large) size*
mūniō, -īre, -īvī, -ītus, *to fortify*
mūnītiō, mūnītiōnis, f., *fortification, rampart*
mūrus, -ī, m., *wall*

N

nam, conj., *for, because*

nancīscor, -ī, nactus sum, *to find*
nāvis, nāvis, nāvium, f., *ship*
nē, conj. + subjn., *so that . . . not, not to*
nē . . . quidem, *not even*
nec, conj., *nor, and . . . not*
necessāriō, adv., *perforce, by necessity*
necessārius, -a, -um, *necessary*
nēmō, nēminis, m., *no one*
neque, conj., *nor, and . . . not*
    neque . . . neque, *neither . . . nor*
Nerviī, -ōrum, m. pl., *the Nervii*
nihil, indecl. noun, *nothing;* **adv.,** *not at all*
nisi, conj., *unless, if . . . not*
noceō, -ēre, nocuī, nocitūrus + dat., *to harm, do harm (to)*
noctū, adv., *at night*
nōn, adv., *not; no*
    nōn sōlum . . . sed etiam, *not only . . . but also*
nōnnūllī, -ae, -a, *some*
noster, nostra, nostrum, *our*
    nostrī, -ōrum, *our men , our soldiers*
novus, -a, -um, *new*
    novissimum agmen, *rear line*
    novissimī, -ōrum, m. pl., *rear-guard*
nox, noctis, noctium, f., *night*
nūllus, -a, -um, *no, none*
numerus, -ī, m., *number*
nūntiō, -āre, -āvī, -ātus, *to announce, report*

O

occīdō, -ere, occīdī, occīsus, *to kill*
occultus, -a, -um, *concealed*
occurrō, -ere, occurrī + dat., *to meet; to attack*
oculus, -ī, m., *eye*
offerō, offerre, obtulī, oblātus, irreg., *to offer, present*
officium, -ī, n., *duty, task, mission*
omnis, -is, -e, *all, the entire; each; every*
oppidum, -ī, n., *town, stronghold*
opportūnus, -a, -um, *well-placed*
opus, operis, n., *building, fortifying*

ōrdō, ōrdinis, m., *rank*

P

pāgus, -ī, m., *clan*
pār, paris, *equal*
parātus, -a, -um, *prepared, ready*
parō, -āre, -āvī, -ātus, *to prepare*
pars, partis, f., *part; side; direction*
passus, -ūs, m., *step, pace*
pater, patris, m., *father*
paucī, -ae, -a, *a few*
paulātim, adv., *gradually*
paulum, -ī, n., *a little*
paulum, adv., *a little, somewhat*
pāx, pācis, f., *peace*
pellō, -ere, pepulī, pulsus, *to rout*
per, prep. + acc., *through*
perīculum, -ī, n., *danger*
perpaucī, -ae, -a, *very few*
perspiciō, -ere, perspexī,
    perspectus, *to see clearly*
persuādeō, -ēre, persuāsī, persuā-
    sus + dat., *to persuade, convince*
perturbō, -āre, -āvī, -ātus, *to throw
    into confusion; to disturb, upset*
perveniō, -īre, pervēnī, perventūrus
    + ad + acc., *to arrive at, reach*
pēs, pedis, m., *foot*
petō, -ere, petīvī, petītus, *to seek; to
    ask (for)*
phalanx, phalangis, f., *phalanx*
pīlum, -ī, n., *javelin*
Pīsō, Pīsōnis, m., *Piso*
plērumque, adv., *generally, usually;
    often*
populus, -ī, m., *people, nation*
porta, -ae, f., *gate*
possum, posse, potuī, irreg., *to be
    able, can*
post, prep. + acc., *after, behind*
posteā, adv., *afterwards, later*
postquam, conj., *after*
postrīdiē, adv., *on the day after*
praesidium, -ī, n., *guard*
praestō, -āre, praestitī, praestātus,
    to perform
praesum, praeesse, praefuī, irreg. +

dat., *to be in command (of)*
praetereā, adv., *besides, moreover*
premō, -ere, pressī, pressus, *to press
    hard, bear down on*
prīmus, -a, -um, *first*
    prīmum, adv., *first*
prīnceps, prīncipis, m., *chieftain*
priusquam, conj., *before*
prō, prep. + abl., *in front of*
prōcēdō, -ere, prōcessī,
    processūrus, *to go forward*
procul, adv., *far away, at a distance*
prōcurrō, -ere, prōcurrī, prōcur-
    sūrus, *to rush forward*
proelium, -ī, n., *battle, skirmish*
profectiō, profectiōnis, f., *setting out,
    departure*
proficīscor, -ī, profectus sum, *to set
    out*
prohibeō, -ēre, -uī, -itus, *to prevent*
prōiciō, -ere, prōiēcī, prōiectus, *to
    throw forward, throw*
prōnūntiō, -āre, -āvī, -ātus, *to
    announce, make known*
prope, adv., *near, nearly*
propter, prep. + acc., *because of*
proptereā quod, *because*
proximus, -a, -um, *nearest, closest*
pudor, pudōris, m., *sense of honor*
pugna, -ae, f., *fight, battle*
pugnō, -āre, -āvī, -atūrus, *to fight*

Q

quaerō, -ere, quaesīvī, quaesītus, *to
    seek; to ask*
quam, conj., in comparisons, *than*
quantus, -a, -um, *how great, how
    much*
quārtus, -a, -um, *fourth*
quattuor, *four*
-que, conj., *and*
quī, qua, quod, indefinite adj., *any*
quī, quae, quod, relative
    pronoun, *who, which, that;* interrog.
    adj., *what, which*
quidem, *certainly, at any rate*

quīnam, quaenam, quodnam,
emphatic interrog. adj., *what*
quis, quid, interrog. pronoun, *who,*
what
quisque, quaeque, quidque, *each*
quō, adv., *to where, where;* conj. +
subjn., *in order that, so that*
quod, conj., *because*
quod sī, *but if*
quoque, adv., *also, too*

R

ratiō, ratiōnis, f., *plan; method*
recipiō, -ere, recēpī, receptus + **sē**,
to retreat, withdraw
redintegrō, -āre, -āvī, -ātus, *to renew,*
revive
relinquō, -ere, relīquī, relictus, *to*
leave behind, leave
reliquus, -a, -um, *remaining, the rest*
of
repente, adv., *suddenly*
reperiō, -īre, repperī, repertus, *to*
find, discover
rēs, reī, f., *thing, matter; situation*
rēs frūmentāria, *grain supply*
rem gerere, *to fight (a battle)*
respondeō, -ēre, respondī,
respōnsus, *to respond, reply*
restituō, -ere, restituī, restitūtus, *to*
restore, revive, renew
retineō, -ēre, retinuī, retentus, *to*
retain, keep
Rhēnus, -ī, m., *the Rhine River*
rīpa, -ae, f., *bank, shore*
Rōmānus, -a, -um, *Roman;* m. pl., *the*
Romans
rūrsus, adv., *again*

S

saepenumerō, adv., *very often,*
frequently
salūs, salūtis, f., *safety, survival*
satis, adv. or substantive, *enough*
scūtum, -ī, n., *shield*
sē, *himself, herself, itself, themselves*
sed, conj., *but*

Sēquanī, -ōrum, m. pl., *the Sequani*
sequor, sequī, secūtus sum, *to follow*
sēsē, alternate form of **sē**
sex, *six*
sī, conj., *if*
quod sī, *but if*
sīc, adv., *thus, so, to such a degree*
signum, -ī, n., *sign, signal; military*
standard
signa ferre, *to advance*
silva, -ae, f., *woods, forest*
sine, prep. + abl., *without*
singulī, -ae, -a, *single, individual*
speciēs, -ēī, f., *sight; appearance*
spērō, -āre, -āvī, -ātus, *to hope*
spēs, -eī, f., *hope, expectation, prospect*
statuō, -ere, statuī, statūtus, *to decide*
subeō, -īre, subiī, subitus, irreg., *to*
come up, approach
subitō, adv., *suddenly*
subsequor, -ī, subsecūtus sum, *to*
follow close behind
subsidium, -ī, n., *reinforcement;*
support, help
sum, esse, fuī, futūrus, irreg., *to be*
summittō, -ere, summīsī,
summissus, *to send help*
summus, -a, -um, *highest; greatest*
superior, superior, superius, gen.,
superiōris, *higher*
superō, -āre, -āvī, -ātus, *to be*
superior; to defeat, conquer
sustineō, -ēre, sustinuī, sustentus,
to hold up; to withstand
suus, -a, -um, *his, her, its, their*
sua, n. pl., *one's possessions*
suōs, m. pl., *their men, their*
soldiers; his men, his soldiers

T

tam, adv., *so*
tamen, adv., *however, nevertheless*
tantus, -a, -um, *such, so great*
tēlum, -ī, n., *weapon* (for hurling)
temptō, -āre, -āvī, -ātus, *to try*
tempus, temporis, n., *time*
ūnō tempore, *at one time,*

simultaneously

teneō, -ēre, tenuī, tentus, *to hold*

tergum, -ī, n., *back*

    ā tergō or **post tergum,** *from behind*

    tergum vertere, *to flee*

terra, -ae, f., *land, ground*

tertius, -a, -um, *third*

Tigurīnī, -ōrum, m. pl., *the Tigurini*

timeō, -ēre, timuī, *to be afraid (of)*

timidus, -a, -um, *fearful, cowardly*

timor, timōris, m., *fear, panic*

Titūrius, -ī, m., *Titurius (Sabinus)*

tollō, -ere, sustulī, sublātus, *to raise*

tōtus, -a, -um, *whole, entire*

trādō, -ere, trādidī, trāditus, *to hand over, deliver, surrender*

trānseō, -īre, trānsiī, trānsitus, irreg., *to go across, cross*

trēs, trēs, tria, trium, *three*

tribūnus mīlitum, tribūnī mīlitum, m., *military tribune*

tum, adv., *then*

turris, turris, turrium, f., *tower*

U

ubi, conj. and adv., *where; when*

ūnā, adv., *together*

unde, adv., *from where*

ūniversus, -a, -um, *all*

ūnus, -a, -um, *one*

    ūnō tempore, *at one time, simultaneously*

urgeō, -ēre, ursī, *to press hard*

usque ad + acc., *as far as, right up to*

ūsus, -ūs, m., *practice, experience*

ut, conj. + indicative, *as;* + subjn., *so that, in order that, that, to*

uter, utra, utrum, *which (of two)*

uterque, utraque, utrumque, *each*

utī, alternate form of **ut**

ūtor, -ī, ūsus sum + abl., *to use*

V

valeō, -ēre, -uī, -itūrus, *to be strong*

vāllum, -ī, n., *wall; rampart*

vehementer, adv., *strongly*

vēndō, -ere, vēndidī, vēnditus, *to sell*

veniō, -īre, vēnī, ventūrus, *to come*

Vercassivellaunus, -ī, m., *Vercassivellaunus*

Vercingetorix, Vercingetorigis, m., *Vercingetorix*

vereor, -ērī, veritus sum, *to fear*

vērō, adv., *truly; even; in fact*

versor, -ārī, versātus sum, + **in** + abl., *to be involved in, be in*

vertō, -ere, vertī, versus, *to turn*

    tergum vertere, *to flee*

videō, -ēre, vīdī, vīsus, *to see*

videor, -ērī, vīsus sum, *to be seen; to seem, appear*

vigilia, -ae, f., (military) *watch*

vir, virī, m., *man*

virtūs, virtūtis, f., *courage, bravery*

vīs, acc., **vim,** abl., **vī,** f., *force; attack;* **vīrēs, vīrium,** f. pl., *strength*

vītō, -āre, -āvī, -ātus, *to avoid*

vīvus, -a, -um, *living, alive*

volō, velle, voluī, irreg., *to wish, want*

vōx, vōcis, f., *voice;* pl., *words*

vulgō, adv., *everywhere*

vulnerō, -āre, -āvī, -ātus, *to wound*

vulnus, vulneris, n., *wound*

vultus, -ūs, m., *face; expression*

CREDITS

Text Credits: All translations of Caesar's *De bello Gallico* are reprinted with permission of David R. Godine, from *Julius Caesar: The Battle for Gaul,* translated by Anne and Peter Wiseman. Translation copyright © 1985 by Anne Wiseman.

Photo Credits: Page 13, Sachsische Landesbibliothek, Dresden; page 21, Hirmer Fotoarchiv, Munich; Page 58, Alinari/Art Resource, NY; page 80, Alinari/Art Resource, NY; page 82, from L'Histoire de France by M. Guizot, copyright © 1875 Libraire Hachette.

Map Credits: Pages v, 6, 12, 34, 35, 56, 64, 74, 78, Martin Walz, Arlington, VA.